Do-It-Yourse

PIANO

BY ALISTAIR WATSON

To access audio and video visit:
www.halleonard.com/mylibrary
Enter Code
1582-8248-9890-2643

ISBN 978-1-7051-0-875-8

Visit Hal Leonard Online at
www.halleonard.com

Contact us:
Hal Leonard
7777 West Bluemound Road
Milwaukee, WI 53213
Email: info@halleonard.com

In Europe, contact:
Hal Leonard Europe Limited
42 Wigmore Street
Marylebone, London, W1U 2RN
Email: info@halleonardeurope.com

In Australia, contact:
Hal Leonard Australia Pty. Ltd.
4 Lentara Court
Cheltenham, Victoria, 3192 Australia
Email: info@halleonard.com.au

Contents

How to Use the Book

This book is designed to get you from the ground to an early intermediate level, where you're comfortable sitting at the instrument and can pick up new pieces and songs and learn them all by yourself. You'll go through all the basic concepts of music notation so that you can confidently read music, with songs that gradually increase in difficulty along the way. With each chapter you learn a new concept, and you'll constantly play new music.

"Little and often" is the best approach with practice. Practicing for an hour every day might be an unrealistic goal if you are a busy person, maybe in full time work. Perhaps you can only manage 15 minutes per day. But this is nevertheless useful. You'd be surprised what you can achieve in 15 minutes of concentration. It might be that the difficult piece you couldn't play on Monday feels a lot easier by Thursday, just from the regular practice you've been able to give. Being able to play regularly is what will give you the best results, even if it's in short bursts.

Do It Yourself: Piano is designed as a self-taught method; you don't need a teacher sitting alongside you. Each concept is presented in a friendly, down-to-earth way, which gives you space and time to discover all the delights of playing the piano all by yourself.

Regular features:

TOOLBOX

This will feature great tips on how to get the best out of your playing.

Piano Talk

This will feature fun facts about the piano.

➔ Do-It-Yourself

This will invite you to challenge yourself further, with ideas that go over and above the printed material of the book. These are optional extras.

We begin with some basics: You will learn a little theory along the way, but each concept is illustrated with musical examples so that you get to practice what you've just learned. There are also periodic **Technique Clinics** that focus on a particular area of piano technique.

Video Lessons, Audio Recordings , and Online Supplements

Many of the concepts contained within this book are personally demonstrated by me, where I explain each topic in detail and play through some of the examples. In addition, many pieces of music in the book have been recorded so that you can hear an example of how it should be played. This is designed to give you immediate feedback. Whenever you see either a video or audio symbol and corresponding number, you can look it up and have a listen. In addition, there are PDFs available that serve as supplements to the content within the book. You can access this content by going to **www.halleonard.com/mylibrary** and inputting the code found on page 1 of this book. Happy playing!

Sitting at the Piano

The Basics of Posture and Hand Position 

First of all, you need a piano stool that is at the correct height. An adjustable piano stool is ideal, but you may have something that works okay. You want to be able to sit up straight with your arms out roughly horizontal in front of you. Good posture is important because if you sit with a hunched back, or peering forward at the music, you will quickly get tired.

TOOLBOX

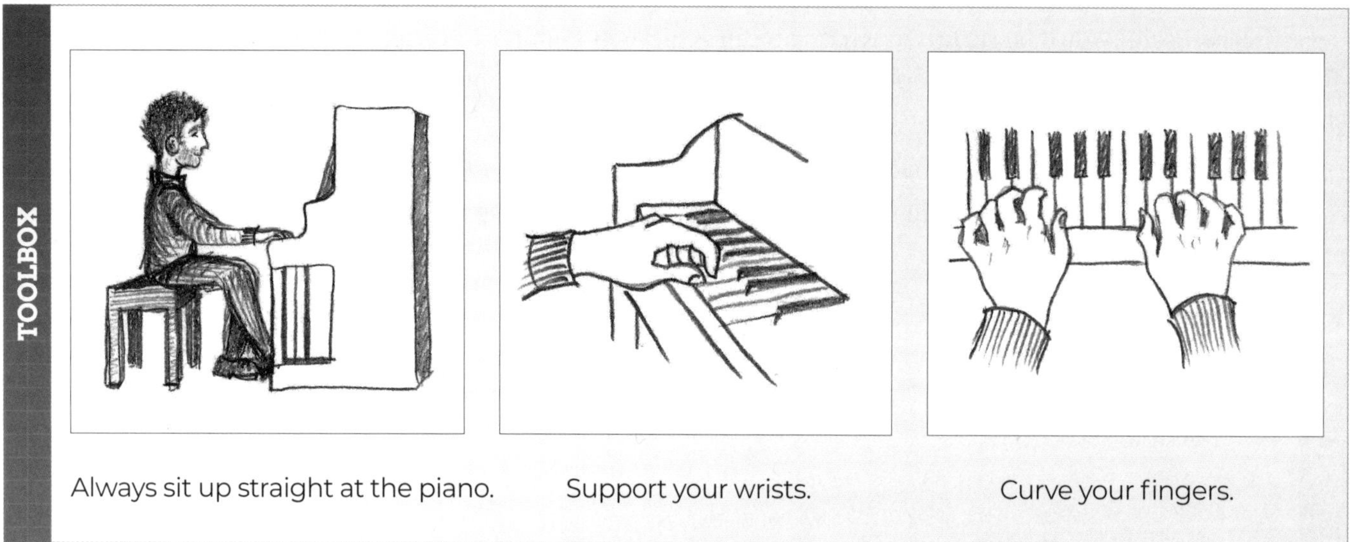

Always sit up straight at the piano. Support your wrists. Curve your fingers.

Secondly, your hands should always be curved, and your wrist should be supported. Imagine you're holding a tennis ball, and the ball is sitting on the keys of the piano. Your hand should always have this curved shape when playing the piano. If the ball is sitting on the keys of the piano, then your forearm is raised slightly. If you remember to hold your wrist in this position when playing, then you have maximum facility at the keyboard. Otherwise, if your fingers are too flat and your wrist is hanging down, you will find it much harder to play.

TOOLBOX

You may have a grand piano, an upright piano, or an electronic keyboard at your home. Ideally, to learn piano, you should have an acoustic piano with 88 keys, but even if you have an electronic instrument with fewer keys (at least 61), the material in this book will get you started.

Piano Talk
The piano was invented in Italy in 1709 by harpsichord maker Bartolomeo di Francesco Cristofori.

Keyboard Geography

Acquainting Yourself with the Keyboard Layout

The keyboard's 88 keys go from low (left) to high (right). Do you notice the way the black keys are grouped in twos and threes? This helps us navigate. Now find the note down to the left of the group of two black notes closest to the middle of the keyboard. This is called **middle C**. This is where we will start. Without this simple, repeating pattern, playing the piano would be impossible, and we would have no idea what the notes are! This pattern imposes order and structure on the keyboard. You can tell where all the Cs are because they always occur at the same point within the sequence.

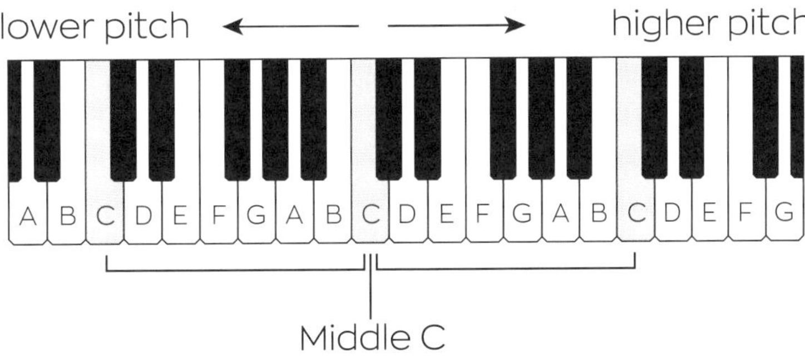

The Musical Alphabet

The musical alphabet has seven letters: A, B, C, D, E, F, and G. After G, we go back to A. There's no H! Starting at middle C, find all the Cs up and down the keyboard. Notice how they sound the same, i.e., they are all the "same note?"

Now do the same with Ds, Es, etc. This pattern repeats itself seven times across the keyboard.

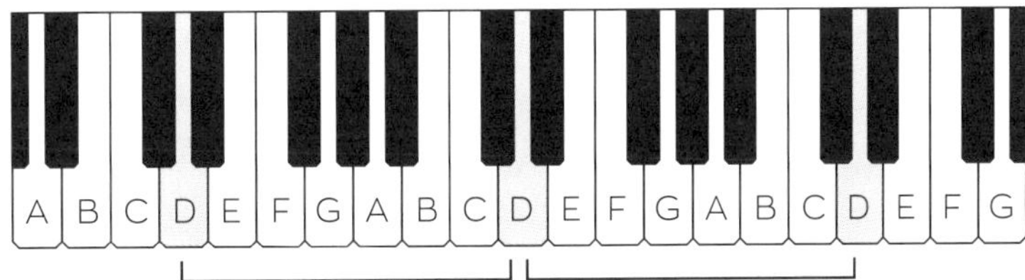

Each group from C to C, D to D, or E to E is known as an **octave**.

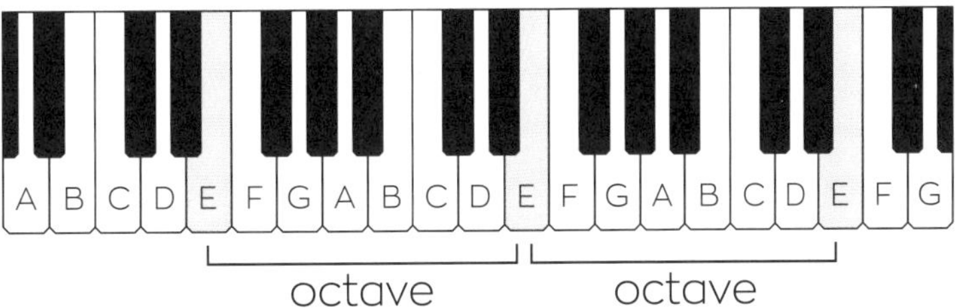

The Building Blocks of Music

Music Notation

The basic principle of written music is that moving from left to right represents the passage of time (like the way we read words) and the notes move up and down, i.e., higher or lower in pitch. This chapter deals just with pulse and rhythm.

The Beat

We often talk about the pulse of a piece of music. What this means is that there is a **beat** underpinning the notes, a bit like a heartbeat. It should be something that you can instinctively feel when you listen to any piece of music. Play some music right now from your stereo or other device. Listen to some fast music and some slow music. As you listen, try to tap the beat on your knee with your hand. This is the "pulse," and it is always there, giving structure to the music. The pulse may speed up during a piece, perhaps to indicate the increase of tension. Or, it may slow down, the beats becoming gradually further apart and eventually stop altogether, at the end of the piece.

Measures

In a piece of music, we divide up time into small units called **measures**. Although there can be any number of measures in a piece, each measure is the same length. This is for convenience, and it makes the music easier to understand. Whatever the notes and rhythms, they sit within this clearly defined structure.

Listen to some music again. As you listen, see if you can hear where the "strong" beats are and where the "weak" beats are. You'll probably find that there is a strong beat, perhaps every four beats or so. Let's call this, "beat 1." Follow the diagram below, and try to match it to what you can hear.

1 2 3 4 | 1 2 3 4 | 1 2 3 4 | 1 2 3 4 | etc. ||

Note Values

Here are the basic note values:

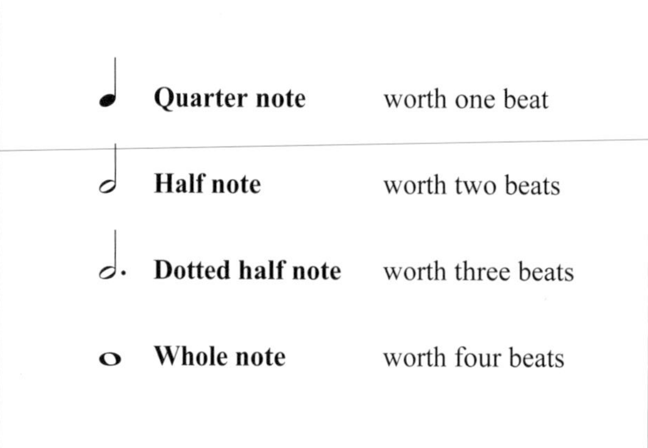

Time Signatures

At the beginning of a piece of written music, there are some of numbers that tell us how to count the beats. This is called a **time signature**. The most common time signature is 4/4. Many classical pieces and almost all pop songs are in 4/4. This is also known as the **meter**. The top note is the most important; this tells you how many beats there are per measure. The bottom note tells you what sort of beat you're counting. To begin with, the bottom note will always be "4." This means we're counting quarter notes.

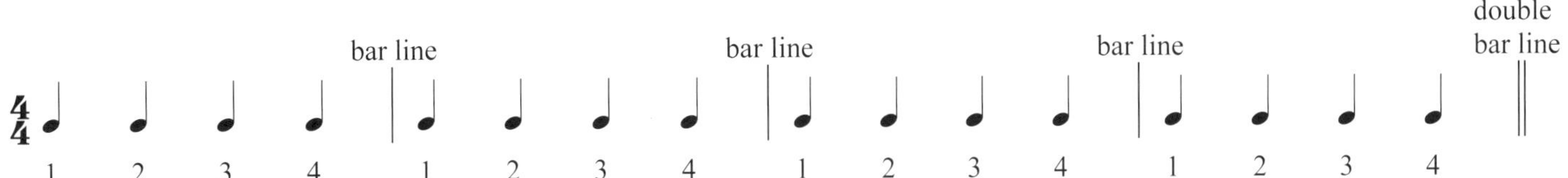

The following are examples of different time signatures. Pay close attention to the top number.

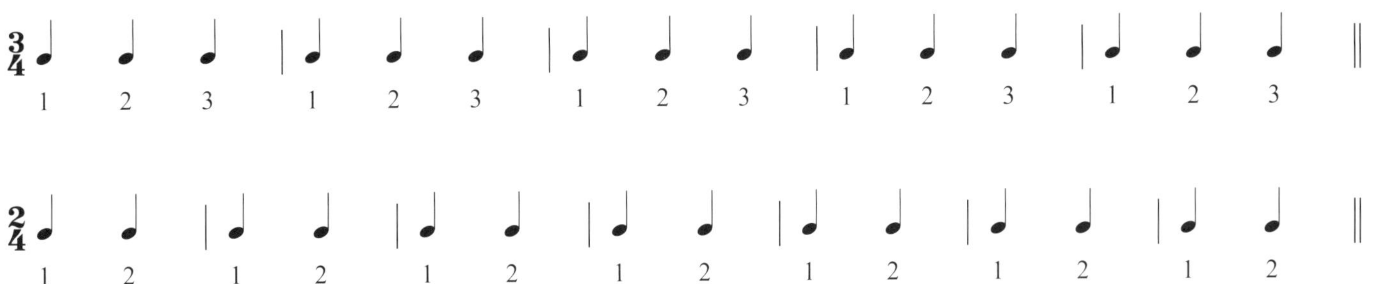

Measures can be filled with any kind of note value, so long as the total number of beats adds up to the top number in the time signature, i.e., all measures will be the same length. Different combinations of note values are what we refer to as **rhythm**. (We will explore more on this in the next chapter.)

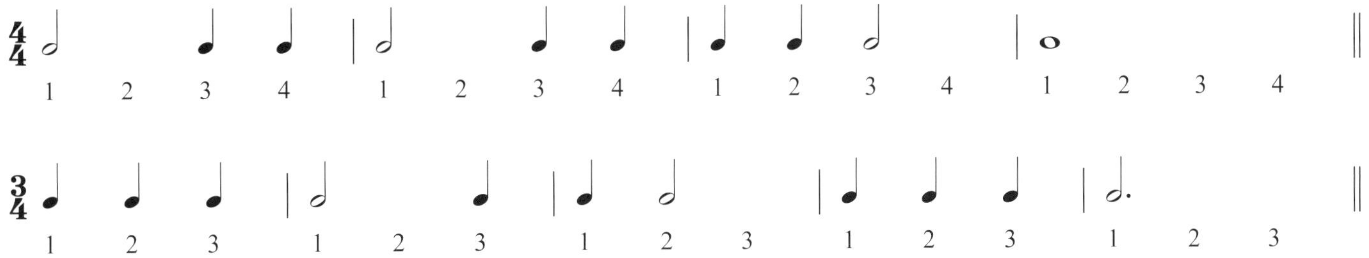

TOOLBOX

Count the beats of the measure rather than the individual beats of each note.

Piano Talk

A typical piano has about 230 steel strings. These must be strung extremely tight to produce sound. Each string usually holds around 168 pounds of tension, making the total tension of most standard pianos just under 20 tons!

The Treble Clef

Let's Get the Right Hand Going

Music is notated on a pattern of five lines called the **staff** or **stave**. Notes are printed either on the lines or in the spaces between. In the left-hand margin of each line we have a clef: the **treble clef** (mostly right hand) at the top and the **bass clef** (mostly left hand) at the bottom.

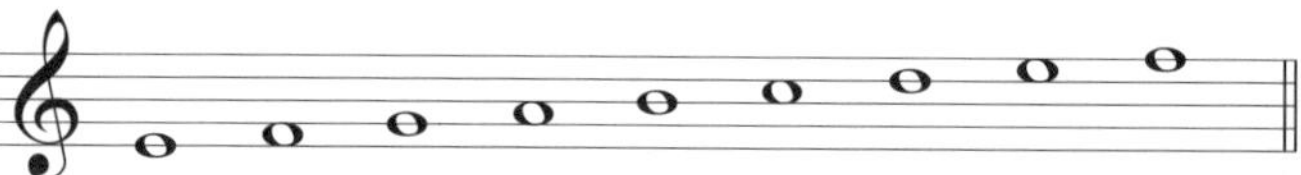

Middle C

Middle C is on its very own line. In the treble clef, it is one line below the staff. Find middle C on the keyboard (look at the diagram in *Keyboard Geography* on page 6) and play it with your thumb.

Next to middle C we have D, then E, F, and G (going higher in pitch and to the right on the keyboard). Look at the following group of notes. Work out where they are on the keyboard and play them with your right hand. If you start with your thumb on middle C, you should end up with your little finger on the G in the following line of music:

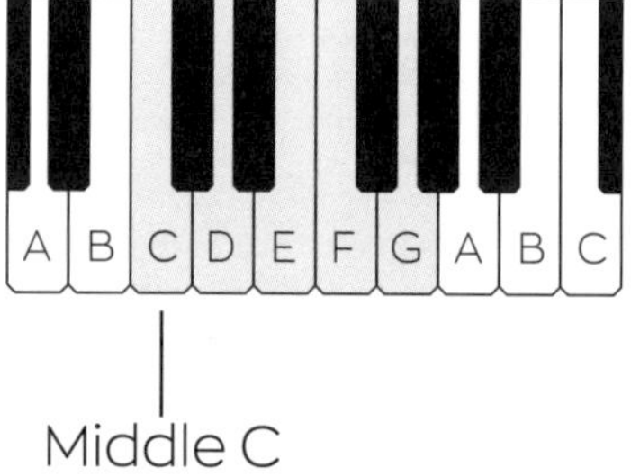

Fingering

For convenience, we number our fingers 1 (thumb), 2, 3, 4, and 5 (little finger). This is a way of making sure we place our hands in the correct starting position. It may seem obvious here, but as we start to play more complex musical patterns in different places on the keyboard, it will become more important.

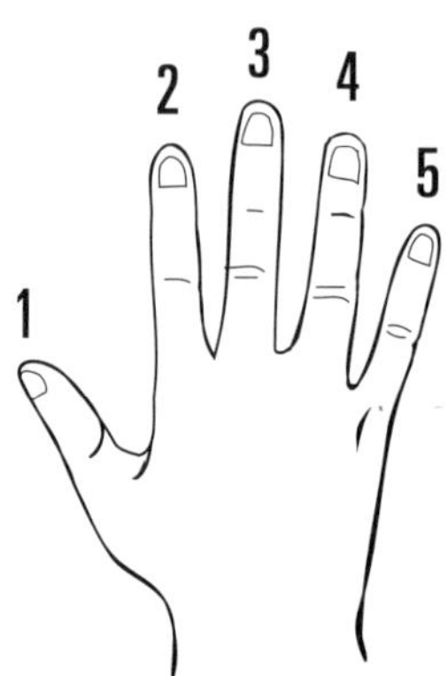

Right-Hand Drill

Start by placing your right hand on the keyboard so that your thumb is on
This means your fifth finger will be on G. The adjacent diagram illustrates th
of your hand, with middle C highlighted.

 *Track 1*

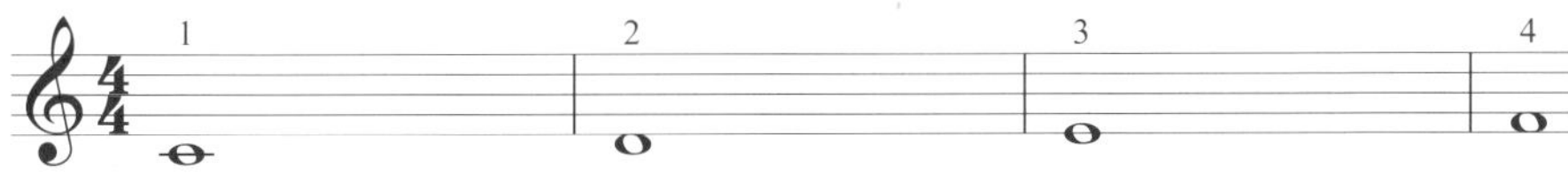

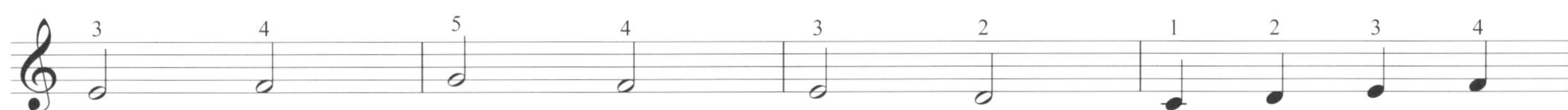

Play this exercise as a warm-up when you sit down to practice the piano.

Piano Talk
The piano has over 10,000 moving parts.

TOOLBOX
Always try to play "next-door" notes with "next-door" fingers: C = 1, D = 2, E = 3, F = 4, and G = 5.

Skipping a Note

The convention is to skip a finger if you skip a note. If you move from C to E, you will use fingers 1, then 3. This enables you to keep your hand in a comfortable, curved position.

 *Track 2*

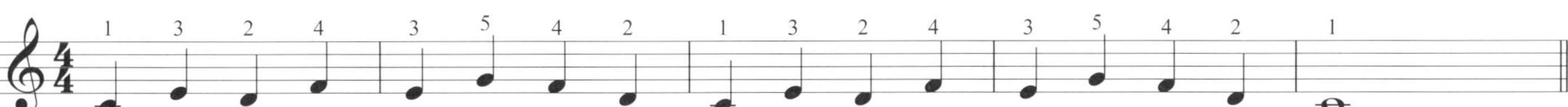

es for the Right Hand

ting Going with Your Playing

We'll start with short tunes notated around middle C. The fingering is marked above the notes, and the counting is marked below.

With each one you should "count yourself in" by counting "1, 2, 3, 4" before you begin. Then, try to keep a count going in your head as you play. This is how you establish the beat, and it then becomes an internal clock, ticking away like a heartbeat. The music stops when you reach the **double bar line** at the end.

The Basics
Time Signature: 4/4 (four quarter notes per measure)
Starts on: First beat. Count, "1, 2, 3, 4," and then play.
First note: Middle C
Right Hand: Thumb

LEAN ON ME

Words and Music by Bill Withers

Track 3

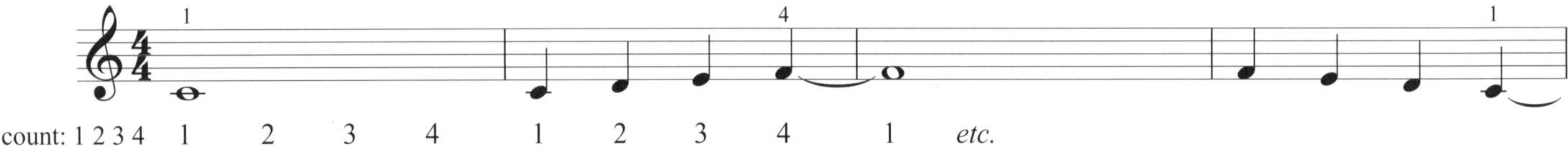

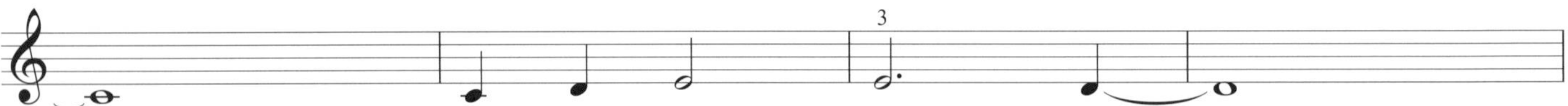

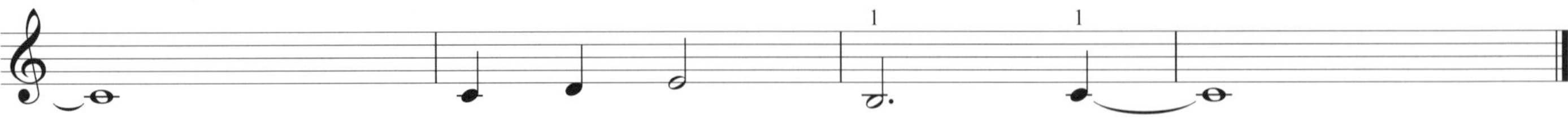

Notice the curved lines underneath some of the notes? These are called **ties**, and they join notes together. We'll deal with ties in greater detail later in the book, but for now, just remember to keep holding the notes down.

TOOLBOX

Tunes don't have to begin on the first beat; they can begin on any beat of the measure. For a song that's in 4/4, there are four possible beats to start on. This affects how you count yourself in. Have a look at the following illustration:

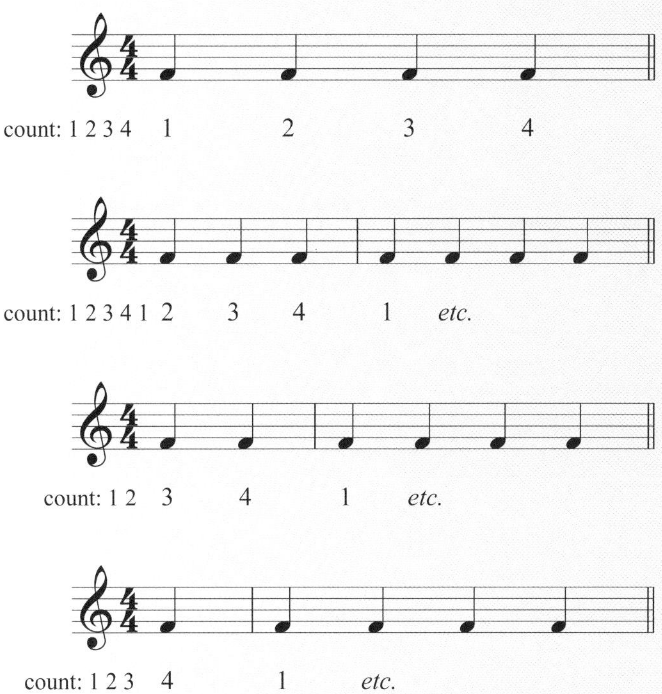

When a piece of music starts on a beat other than beat 1, this means the first measure is incomplete. You will usually find that the last measure of the piece is also incomplete, to make up for it. This happens mostly in classical music.

Here are some well-known tunes that start on different beats of the measure:

- "Happy Birthday" (in 3/4, starts on the third beat),
- "Yellow Submarine" (in 4/4, starts on the fourth beat)
- "Bare Necessities" (in 4/4, starts on the second beat).

Can you think of others?

The Basics
Time Signature: 4/4 (four quarter notes per measure)
Starts on: Third beat. Count, "1, 2," and then play.
First note: G
Right Hand: Fourth finger

HEY JUDE

Words and Music by John Lennon and Paul McCartney

Track 4

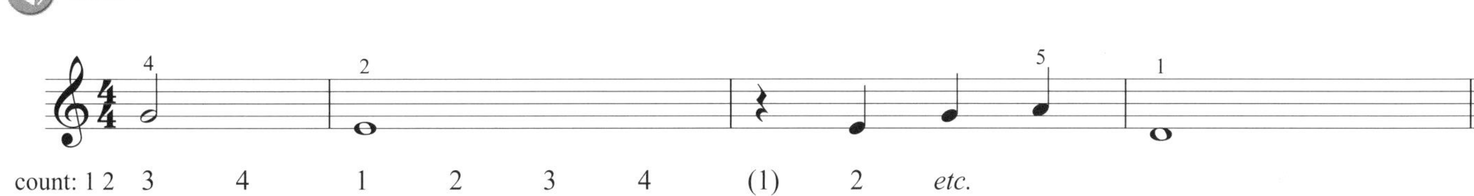

Don't worry about the little squiggle at the start of the third measure. This is a **rest**, which is a short break. (More on rests later in the book.) Both this song and the next begin on the third beat of the measure.

The Basics
Time Signature: 4/4 (four quarter notes per measure)
Starts on: Third beat. Count, "1, 2," and then play.
First note: The next C above middle C
Right Hand: Fifth finger

THEME FROM "JURASSIC PARK"

(from the Universal Motion Picture *Jurassic Park*)

Composed by John Williams

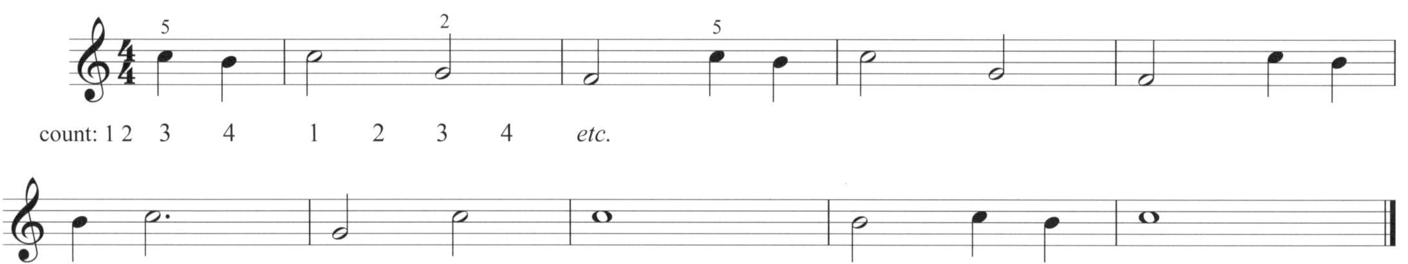

The Basics
Time Signature: 4/4 (four quarter notes per measure)
Starts on: Second beat. Count, "3, 4, 1," and then play.
First note: The next C above middle C
Right Hand: Third finger

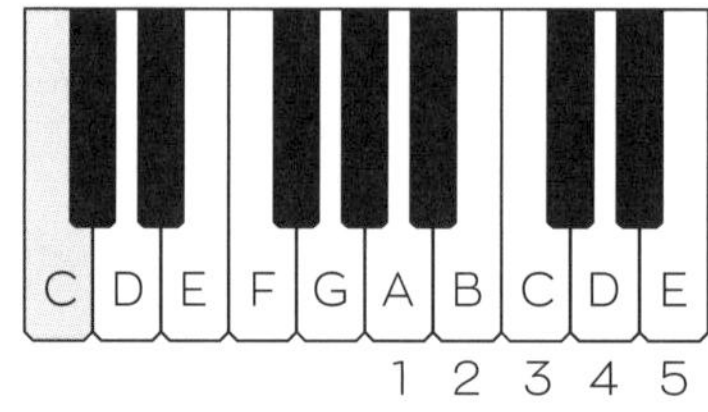

I DREAMED A DREAM

(from *Les Miserables*)

Music by Claude-Michel Schönberg

Lyrics by Alain Boublil, Jean-Marc Natel and Herbert Kretzmer

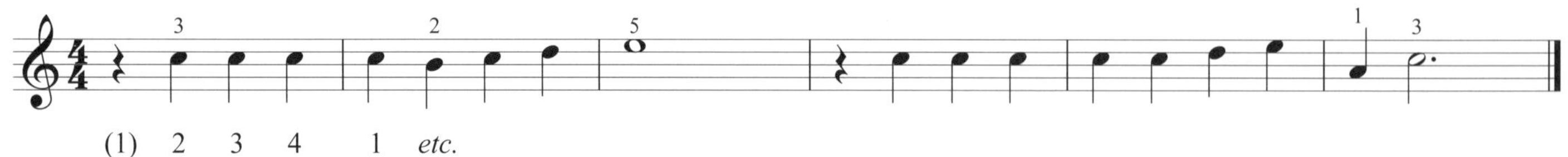

The Basics
Time Signature: 4/4 (four quarter notes per measure)
Starts on: Second beat. Count, "3, 4, 1," and then play.
First note: Middle C
Right Hand: Thumb

WHEN THE SAINTS GO MARCHING IN

American Traditional

(Don't worry about the symbol at the beginning of measure 13; it's another type of rest. For now, just take a break for two beats.)

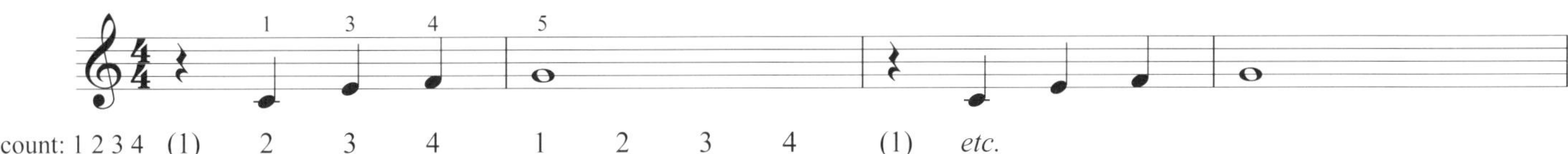

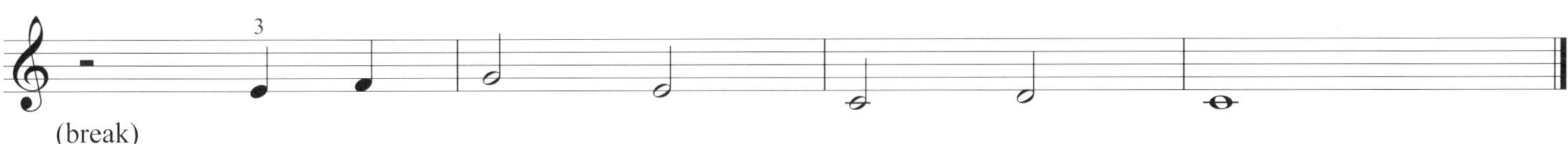

Piano Talk
Most modern pianos have a total of 88 keys: 52 white and 36 black.

The Basics
Time Signature: 4/4 (four quarter notes per measure)
Starts on: Third beat. Count, "1, 2," and then play.
First note: Middle C
Right Hand: Thumb

SPRING
(from *The Four Seasons*)
By Antonio Vivaldi

Track 6

The Bass Clef

Let's Get the Left Hand Going

The staff has the same pattern of lines and spaces, but the bass clef puts everything in a different place. Middle C is on its own line above the staff.

Bass Clef

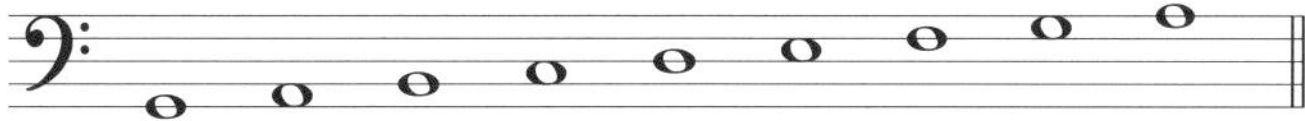

Middle C

Moving from your thumb out to your pinky, the notes below are B, A, then G and F. Remember that after G, we go back to A. So with your left-hand thumb on middle C, look at the following line of music and play these five notes:

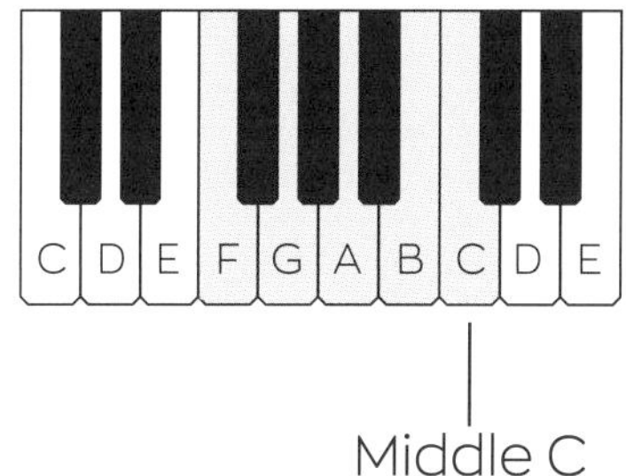

Fingering

The left hand is a mirror image of the right hand, so the fingers are numbered 1 (thumb) to 5 (little finger), but you will need to get used to 1 being at the top.

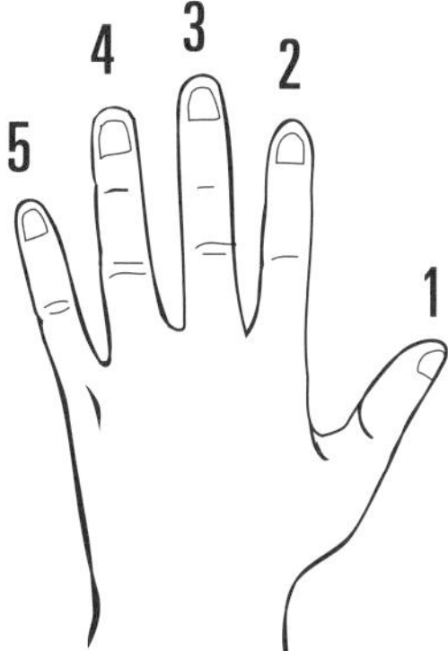

> **Piano Talk**
> The exact middle of a piano keyboard is NOT middle C. It is actually the space between E and F above middle C.

Left-Hand Drill

Place your thumb on middle C and your fifth finger on F.

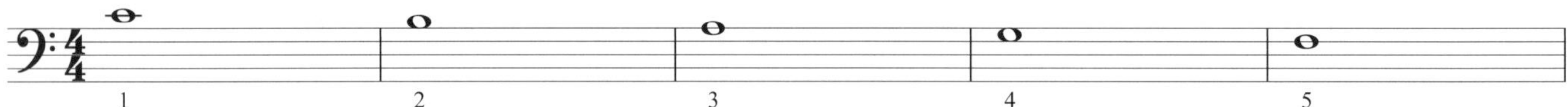

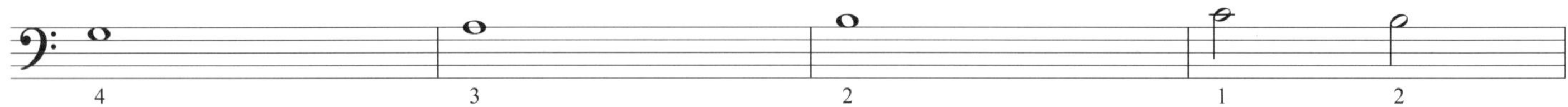

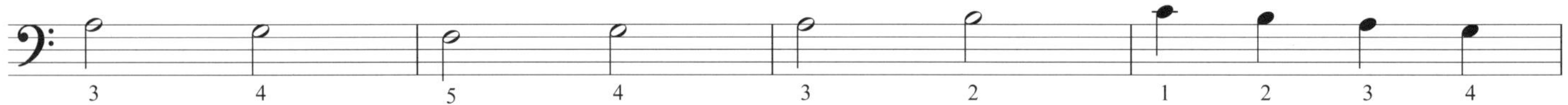

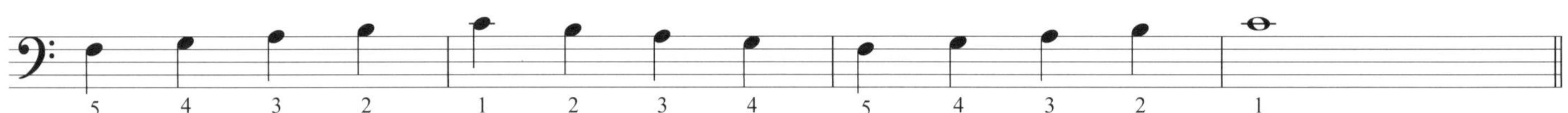

TOOLBOX

Always try to play "next-door" notes with "next-door" fingers: C = 1, B = 2, A = 3, G = 4, and F = 5.

Skipping a Note

The same rules apply: If you skip a note, then skip a finger. This keeps your hand in the correct position.

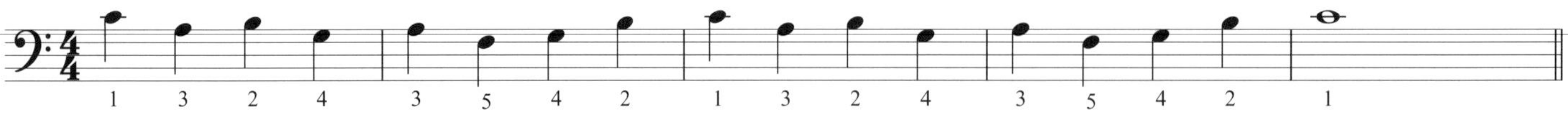

Piano Talk

Piano keys are often referred to as "ivories," but actually, they haven't been made out of ivory (elephant tusks) since the 1940s. Today, they are mostly made from plastic.

Tunes for the Left Hand

For the first tune you have your thumb on middle C, exactly the same position as the previous exercises.

The Basics
Time Signature: 4/4 (four quarter notes per measure)
Starts on: First beat. Count, "1, 2, 3, 4," and then play.
First note: G below middle C
Left Hand: Fourth finger

AU CLAIR DE LA LUNE

French Folksong

Track 9

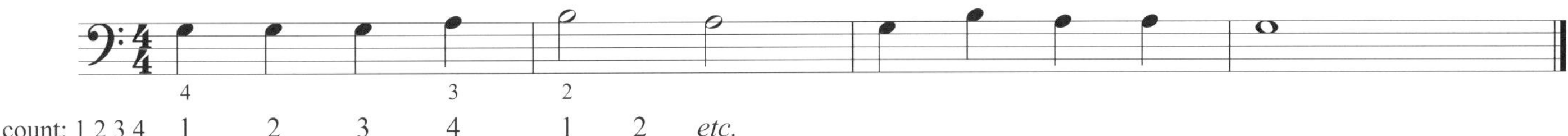

For the next two tunes, you need to move your hand so that your thumb is on D (just above middle C). Check the diagram below.

The Basics
Time Signature: 3/4 (three quarter notes per measure)
Starts on: First beat. Count, "1, 2, 3," and then play.
First note: B below middle C
Left Hand: Third finger

LUCY IN THE SKY WITH DIAMONDS

Words and Music by John Lennon and Paul McCartney

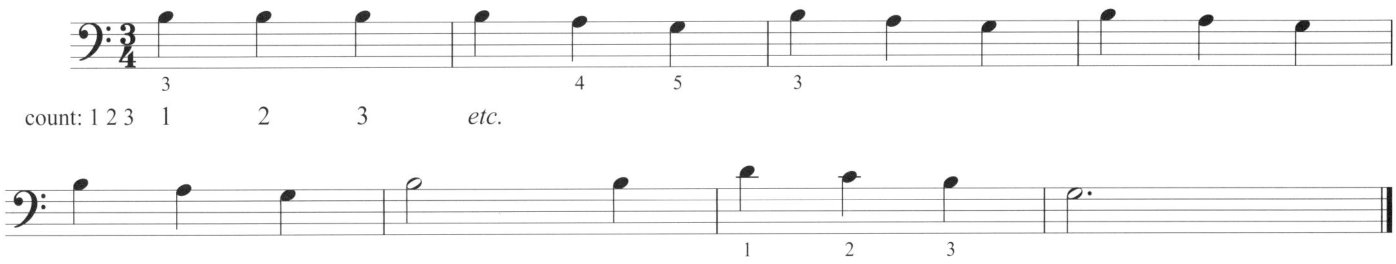

The Basics
Time Signature: 4/4 (four quarter notes per measure)
Starts on: First beat. Count, "1, 2, 3, 4," and then play.
First note: G below middle C
Left Hand: Fifth finger

LOVE ME TENDER

Words and Music by Elvis Presley and Vera Matson

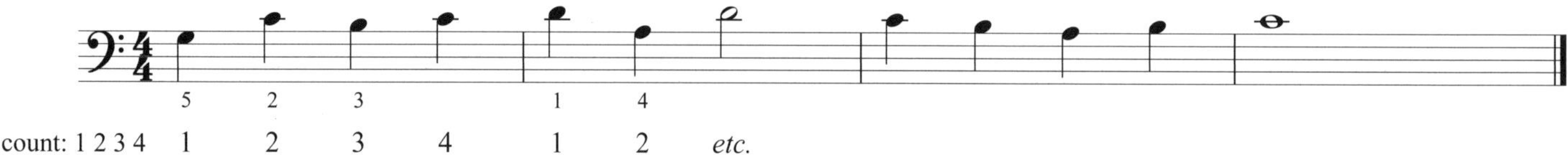

The next tune is a little longer. Here, you need to move your hand lower down the keyboard so that your thumb is above the G and your fifth finger is above the C, an octave below middle C. Check the diagram below.

The Basics
Time Signature: 4/4 (four quarter notes per measure)
Starts on: First beat. Count, "1, 2, 3, 4" and then play.
First note: E below middle C
Left Hand: Third finger

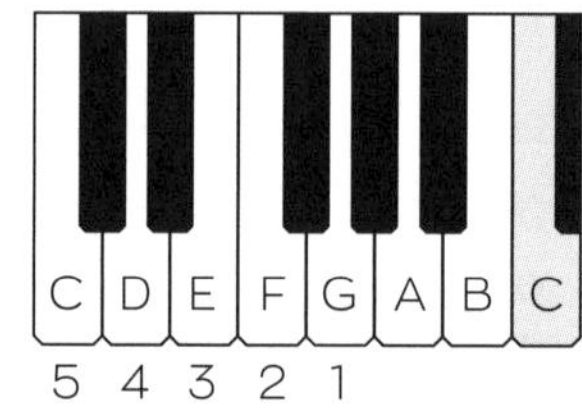

ODE TO JOY

By Ludwig van Beethoven

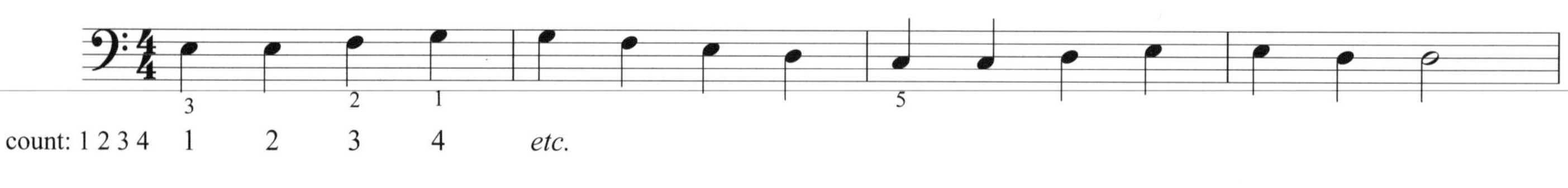

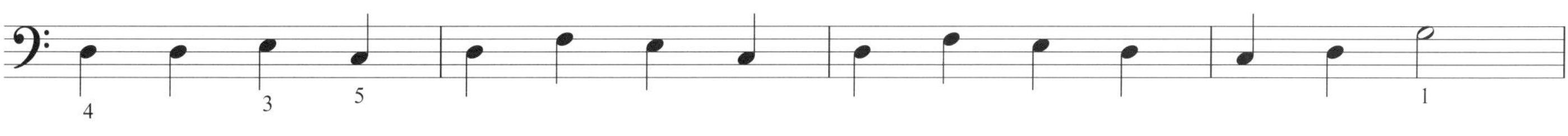

The Basics
Time Signature: 3/4 (three quarter notes per measure)
Starts on: First beat. Count, "1, 2, 3," and then play.
First note: E below middle C
Left Hand: Fourth finger

HALLELUJAH

Words and Music by Leonard Cohen

(Don't worry about the symbol that first occurs in measure 4; it's just another rest. For now, don't play during that measure, but remember to keep counting!)

Track 11

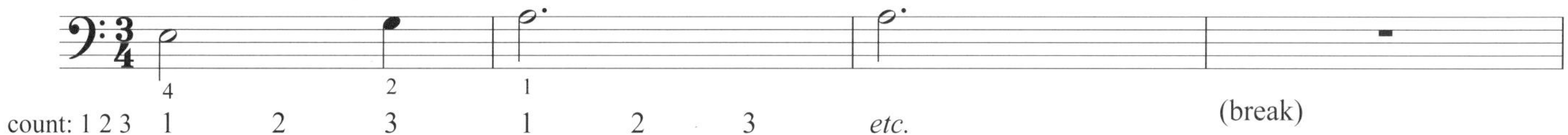

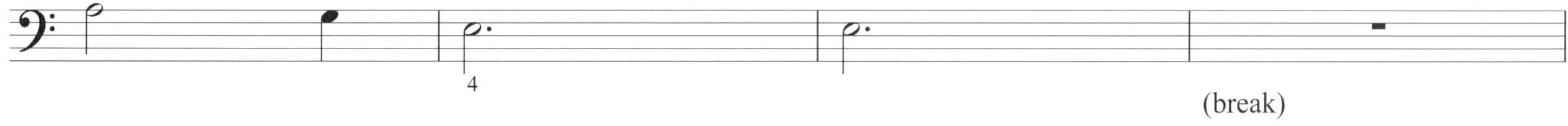

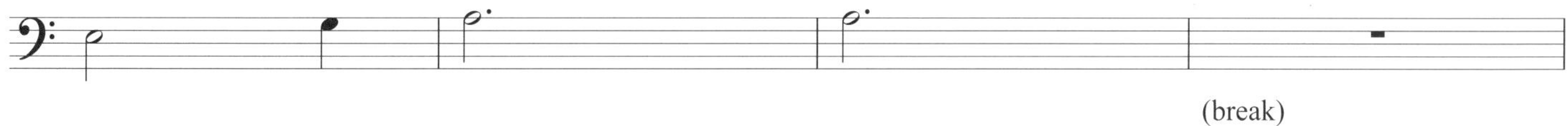

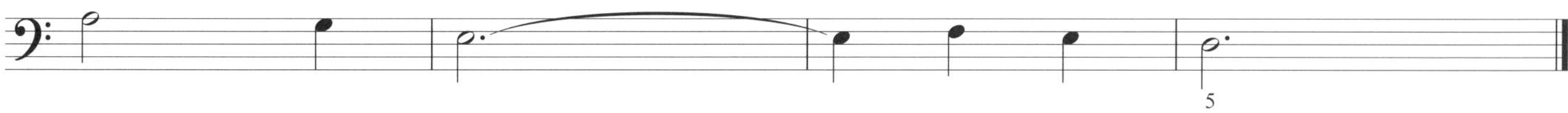

The Basics
Time Signature: 4/4 (four quarter notes per measure)
Starts on: Fourth beat. Count, "1, 2, 3," and then play.
First note: A below middle C
Left Hand: First finger

CLOCKS

Words and Music by Guy Berryman, Jon Buckland, Will Champion and Chris Martin

➔ Do-It-Yourself

If you want to challenge yourself further, try this:

Now that you've done a little playing with each hand, you could go back and play the right-hand songs with the left hand, and then play the left-hand songs with the right hand.

There are two big challenges here:

- You will be playing in the "wrong" clef, i.e., playing with the left hand but reading notes in the treble clef, and vice versa.
- Fingering numbers will all have to change. Instead of 1, you will use 5, etc.

Both these problems can be overcome with a little preparation.

Let's look at "When the Saints Go Marching In": Turn back to page 14 and play this through with your right hand to remind yourself of the notes. Now, to play this with your left hand, you will need to shuffle yourself to the right so that your left hand can comfortably reach the notes above middle C.

Fingering: Instead of 1–2–3–4–5, your hand will be playing 5–4–3–2–1, i.e., your fifth finger will be on middle C and your thumb will be on G.

Here are the first two lines:

Try some of the other songs. Remember that wherever you see fingering number 1, you just have to use 5, and so on.

Now you could try playing the left-hand songs with the right hand. Let's look at "Hallelujah": Turn back to page 19 and play this through with your left hand. Now shuffle over to the left so that our right hand can reach the notes comfortably. Position your hand so that your second finger is on the E and your fifth finger is on the A. Here are the first two lines:

Now try playing the other songs. Remember, this is tricky, and therefore optional! You may wish to come back to this later when you've had a little more experience.

Technique Clinic 1

Exercise Those Fingers!

This is the first of many sections on technique. As your understanding of the piano and reading music increases, so should your ability to play.

One of the biggest obstacles in developing technique is getting all five fingers of each hand to move equally so that you get an even touch at the instrument.

1. Alternating Fingers

Alternate two fingers, playing this quarter-note pattern. Remember to keep your wrist relaxed but supported. Also, try to keep your hand level, keeping your hand from rocking side to side. This is particularly important when you get to fingers 4 and 5.

Track 12

Now do the same with your left hand. This is simply a mirror image of the right-hand exercise, starting on middle C and moving down to F.

Track 13

2. Next-Door Notes

Now we'll broaden out into using all five fingers in a single phrase. Listen for evenness, and try not to move your elbow up as you move towards your fifth finger.

Track 14

R.H.:

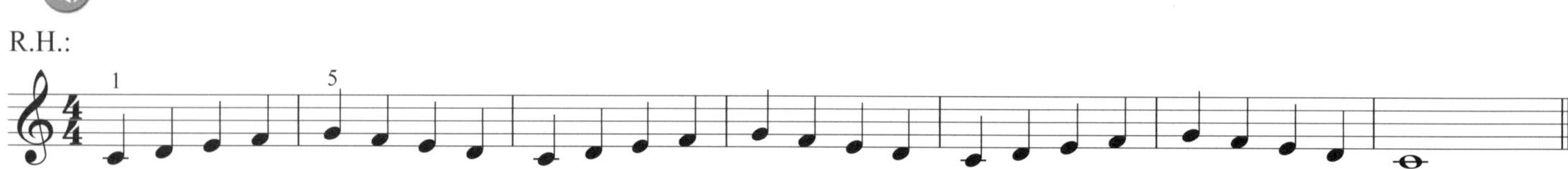

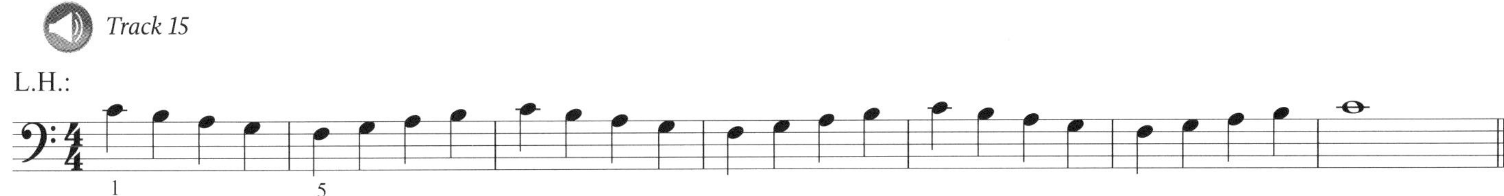

3. Skipping Notes

Move each finger right from the knuckle, again keeping the hand level. Aim for an even touch: all notes should be the same volume.

4. Work Those Weak Fingers

You'll probably find that your fourth and fifth fingers are the weakest in your hand, particularly in your non-dominant hand. This exercise is designed to get right into those areas that need the most attention. Option: Repeat the second measure several times.

And finally, here's a tune that ties all these ideas together:

WOBBLY FINGERS

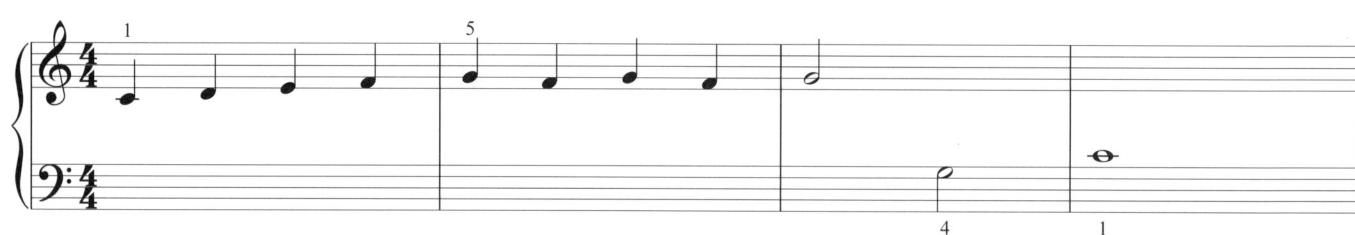

Tunes for Both Hands

The Grand Staff

Now you're ready to put both hands together. We'll start with a handful of simple tunes where the melody line starts in one hand and is passed over to the other. In order to do this, you need to understand the **grand staff**. You've seen musical staves with either the treble clef or the bass clef. When we play with both hands, there are two of these joined together.

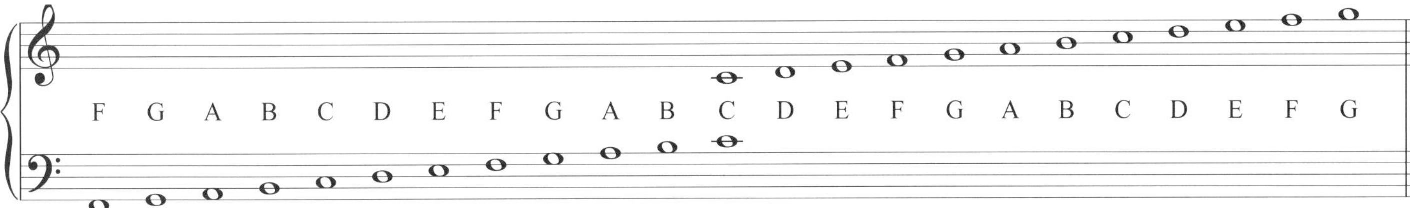

Remember: Middle C is on the line below the treble clef staff and on the line above the bass clef staff.

Pachelbel's *Canon* starts off in the right hand, but at measure 4, it passes over to the left hand. The same thing happens in the third line. Keep in mind that these transitions should be seamless. This also has two **repeat signs:** the two dots on each staff at the end of the line. Play the first line twice before going on.

Hand positions: Both thumbs should be hovering above middle C.

The Basics
Time Signature: 4/4 (four quarter notes per measure)
Starts on: First beat. Count, "1, 2, 3, 4," and then play.
First note: E above middle C
Right Hand: Third finger

Left Hand:

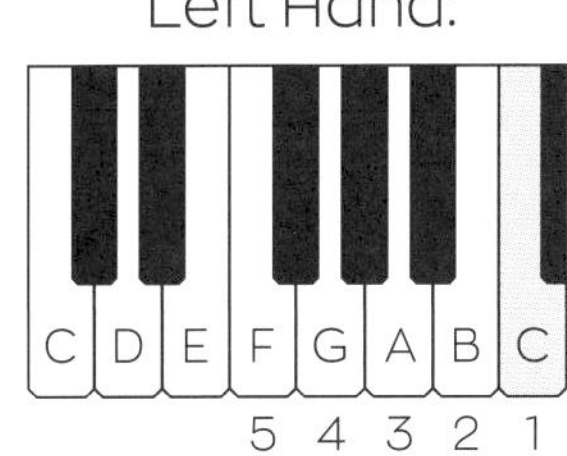

Right Hand:

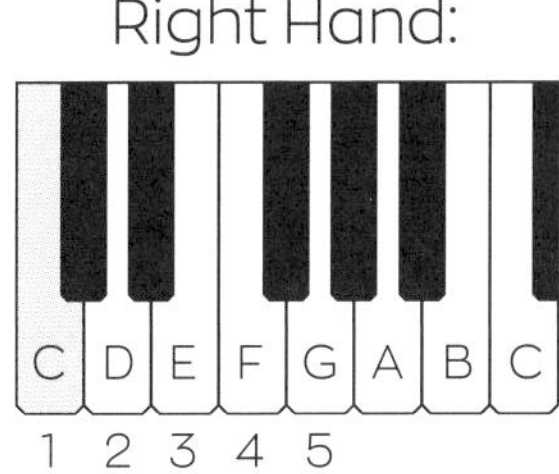

CANON IN D

By Johann Pachelbel

Track 21

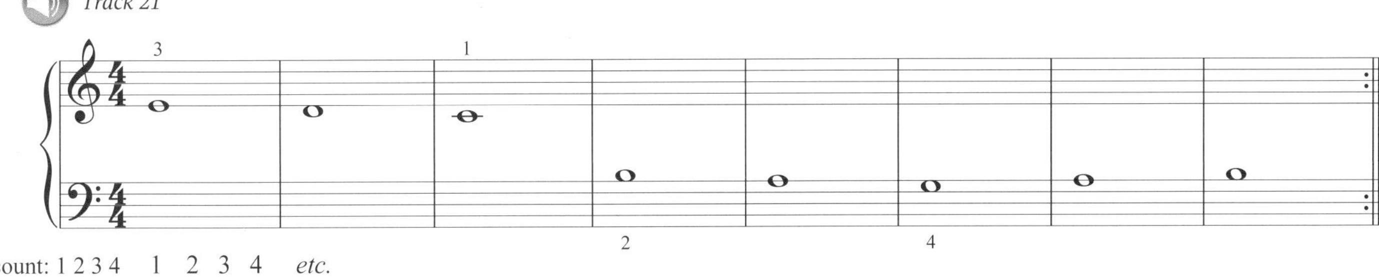

count: 1 2 3 4 1 2 3 4 *etc.*

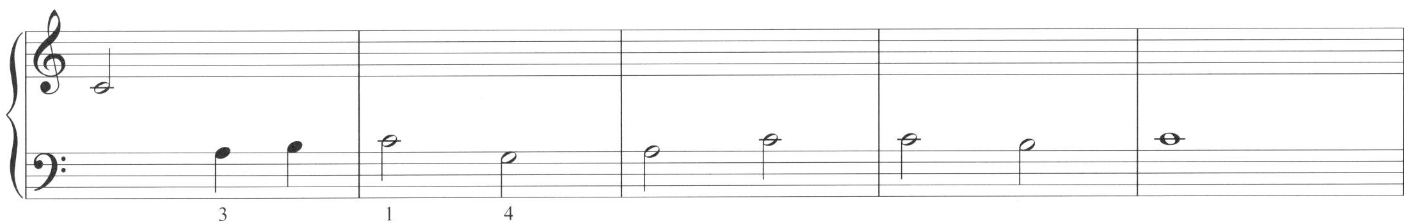

TOOLBOX

Your thumbs now share middle C.

Play with both hands hovering above the keyboard so that you can reach middle C with either thumb. Your arms need to be mobile and free.

In the next song, your hands must really work together. This is especially important when you swap between hands in the middle of a measure, e.g., measure 2.

The Basics
Time Signature: 4/4 (four quarter notes per measure)
Starts on: First beat. Count, "1, 2, 3, 4," and then play.
First note: Middle C
Right Hand: thumb

Left Hand:

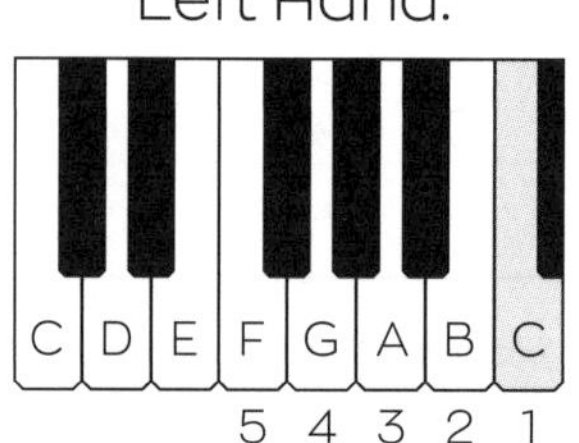

Right Hand:

MY HEART WILL GO ON (LOVE THEME FROM 'TITANIC')

(from the Paramount and Twentieth Century Fox Motion Picture *Titanic*)

Music by James Horner
Lyric by Will Jennings

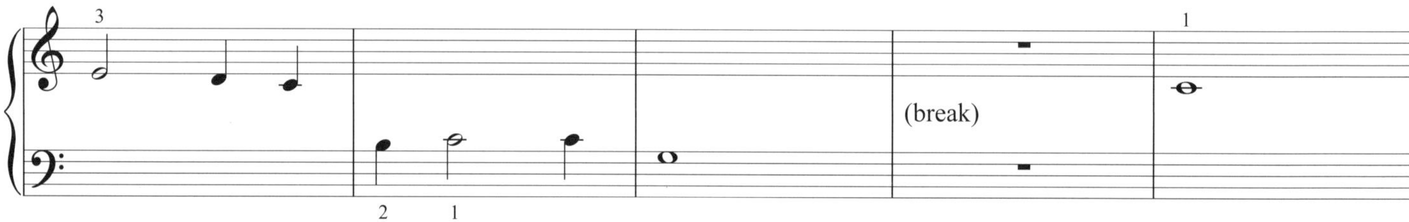

For the next song, your left hand needs to move one note to the right; your thumb is now playing the D above middle C. This means the hands are overlapping a little more, so you need to be prepared to move your hands out of the way in the middle of phrases.

The Basics
Time Signature: 4/4 (four quarter notes per measure)
Starts on: First beat. Count, "1, 2, 3, 4," and then play.
First note: Middle C
Right Hand: Second finger

Left Hand:

Right Hand:

GOOD KING WENCESLAS

Words by John M. Neale
Music from Piae Cantiones

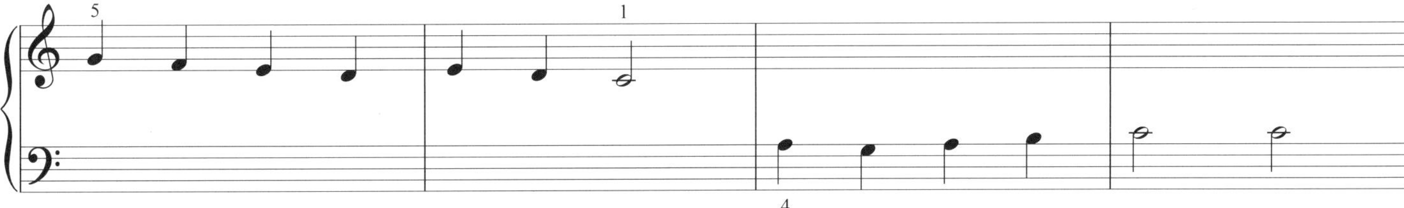

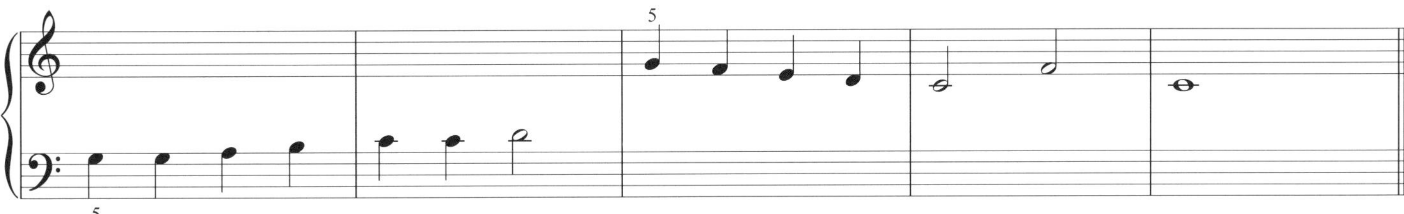

Piano Talk
The piano can be considered both a string and percussion instrument because hammers strike the strings to produce sound.

The Tie

You first met the tie back on page 11 with "Lean On Me"—a curved line underneath two notes. A tie simply joins two notes together. Play the first note and hold it down for the length of both of them added together. The two notes must be the *same note*; otherwise it's known as a **slur**. (More on slurs later.)

In the above example, you would play one middle C and hold it for three beats.

It may be that a composer wants a note to be held on over the barline, like this:

Track 24

Let's return to "When the Saints Go Marching In," which you played back on page 14. Here it is written out again, but with ties added. This means that you simply hold onto the long G both times, into the next measure. Watch out for the really long F, which you must hold down for five beats.

Time Signature: 4/4 (four quarter notes per measure)
Starts on: Second beat. Count, "3, 4, 1," and then play.
First note: Middle C
Right Hand: Thumb

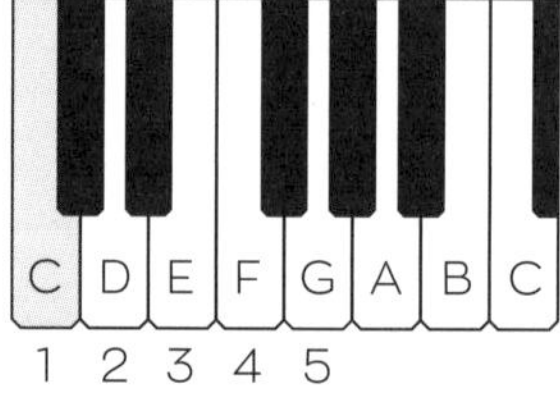

WHEN THE SAINTS GO MARCHING IN

American Tradtional

Track 26

The Basics
Time Signature: 4/4 (four quarter notes per measure)
Starts on: First beat. Count, "1, 2, 3, 4," and then play.
First note: A below middle C
Left Hand: Third finger

Left Hand:

Right Hand:

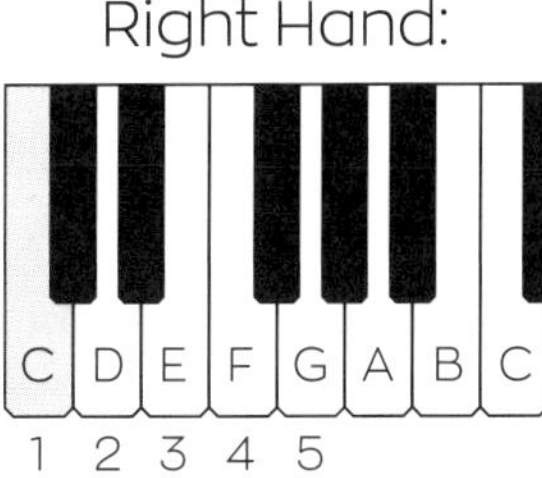

There are lots of ties in this tune, particularly notes that are tied over into the next measure. Just remember to keep counting four beats per measure. If it would help, you could write out the beats underneath.

HELLO

Words and Music by Adele Adkins and Greg Kurstin

Track 27

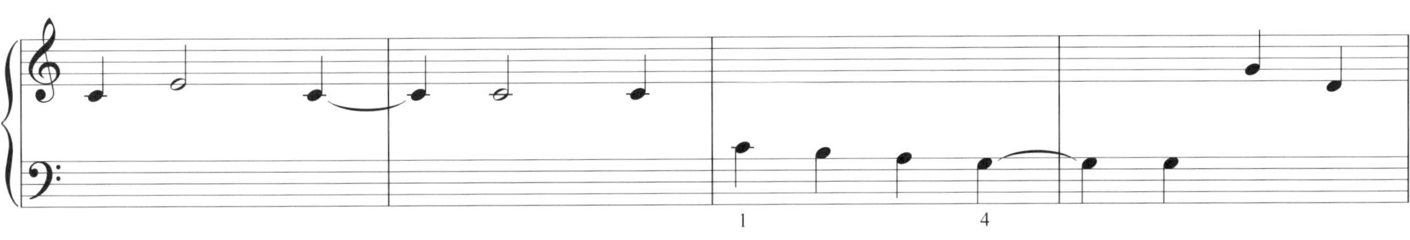

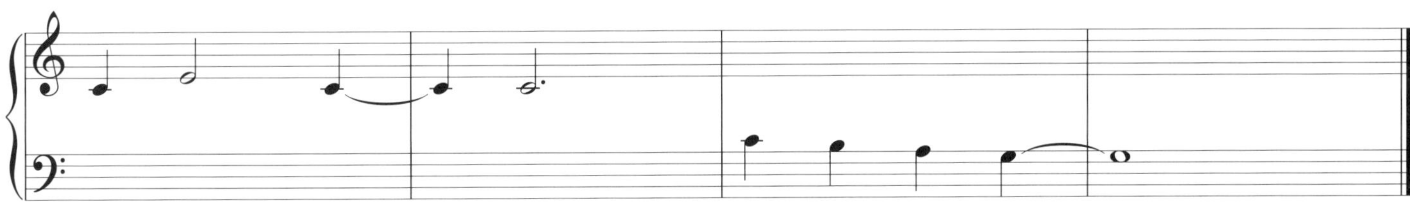

The Basics
Time Signature: 4/4 (four quarter notes per measure)
Starts on: First beat. Count, "1, 2, 3, 4," and then play.
First note: A below middle C
Right Hand: Fifth finger

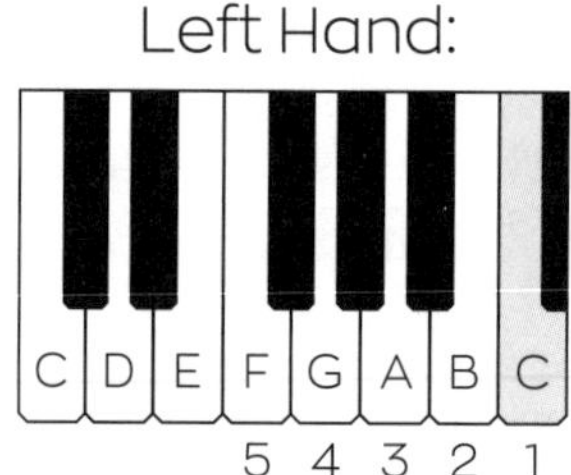

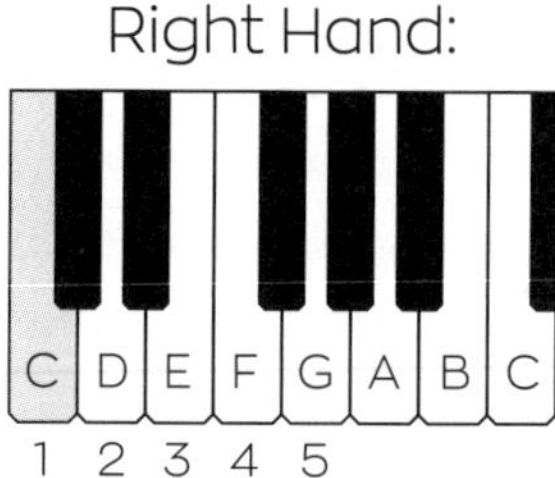

This one is a little harder, as the right hand is positioned one note higher; it will feel very different. The thumbs now have separate notes. There are also a lot of notes tied over the bar line.

SHOTGUN

Words and Music by George Barnett, Joel Laslett Pott and Fred Gibson

count: 1 2 3 4 1 2 3 4 1 *etc.*

This chapter finishes with the longest song you will have played so far. Get used to practicing from the start of a particular phrase, e.g., from measure 17, rather than starting at the beginning each time. This is a good way to get better at a tricky section. Again, notice the ties in this song; you must keep a careful count of four beats in each measure.

The Basics
Time Signature: 4/4 (four quarter notes per measure)
Starts on: Second beat. Count, "3, 4, 1," and then play.
First note: A below middle C
Left Hand: Third finger

Left Hand:

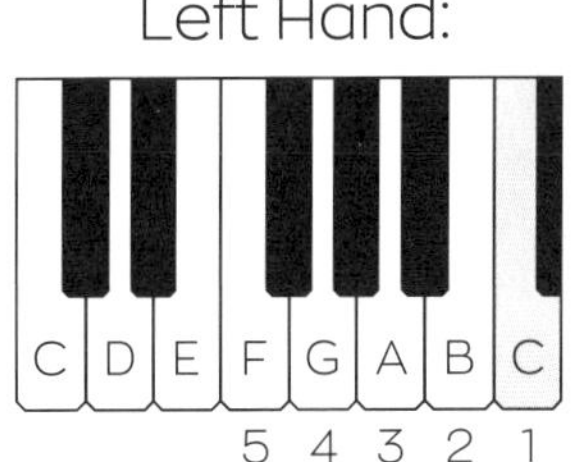

C D E F G A B C
5 4 3 2 1

Right Hand:

C D E F G A B C
1 2 3 4 5

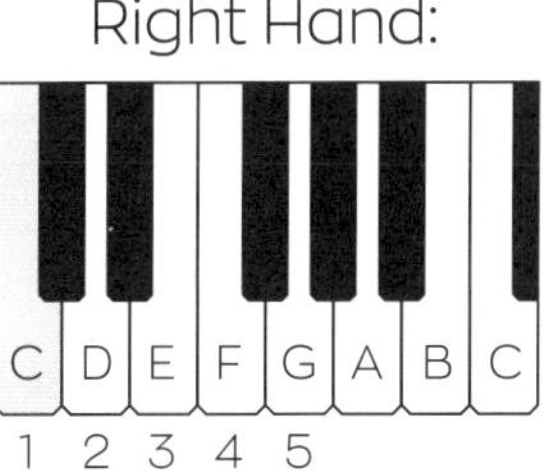

LET IT GO
(from *Frozen*)

Music and Lyrics by Kristen Anderson-Lopez and Robert Lopez

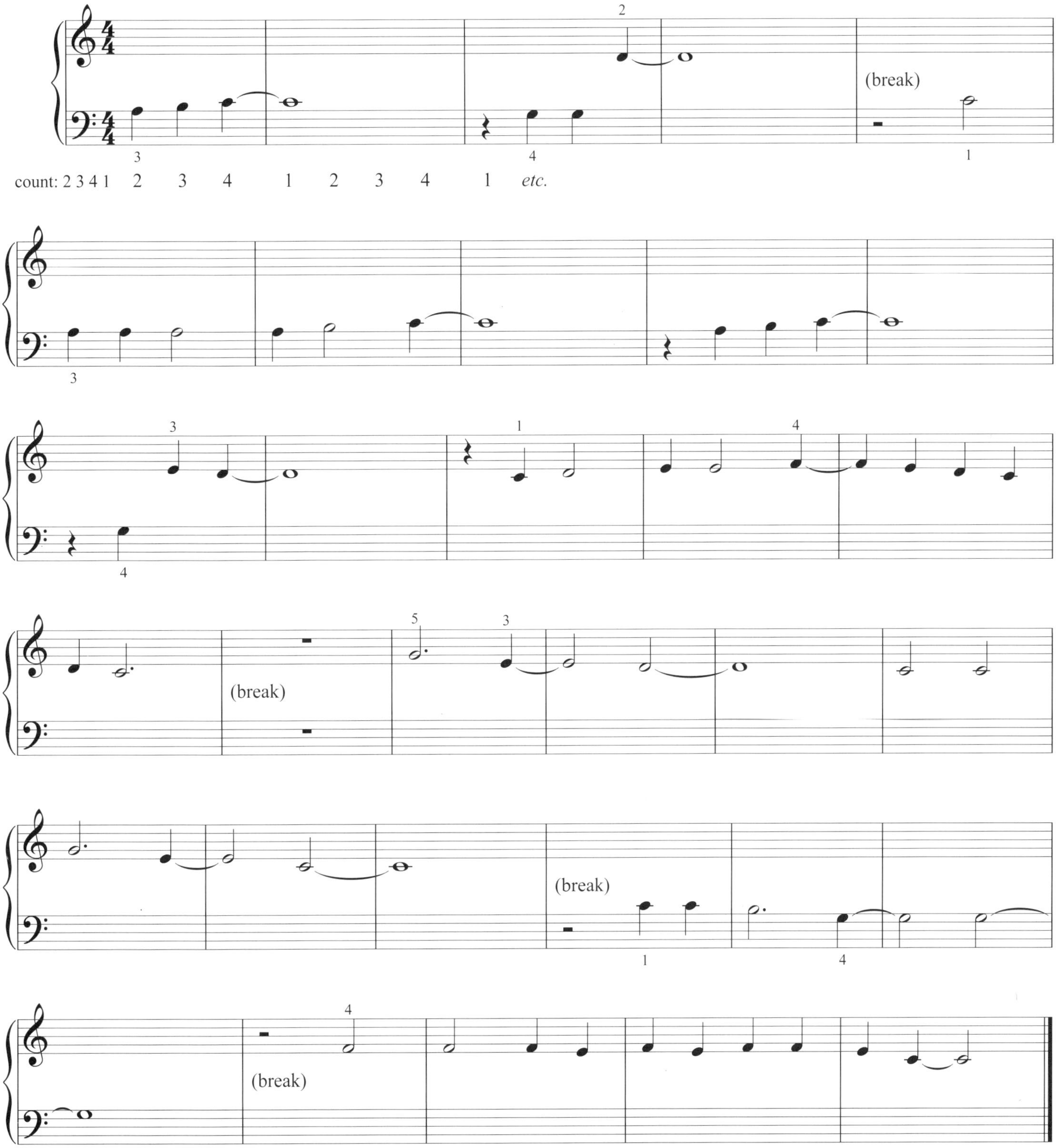
(break)
count: 2 3 4 1 2 3 4 1 2 3 4 1 etc.
(break)
(break)
(break)

Hands Together

Now we'll take another look at some of the tunes you've already played, but this time, we're adding a very simple accompaniment in the left hand. The left hand now provides an outline of harmony.

> **TOOLBOX**
> Always play hands separately first. Only play hands together once you've mastered each hand on its own.

We'll start by returning to "Ode To Joy" by Beethoven. You played this back on page 18 just with the left hand. Here the tune is in the right hand with a very simple accompaniment in the left hand. Both hands remain in a five-finger hand position throughout.

The Basics
Time Signature: 4/4 (four quarter notes per measure)
Starts on: First beat. Count, "1, 2, 3, 4," and then play.
First note: E above middle C
Left Hand: The next C below middle C

Left Hand:

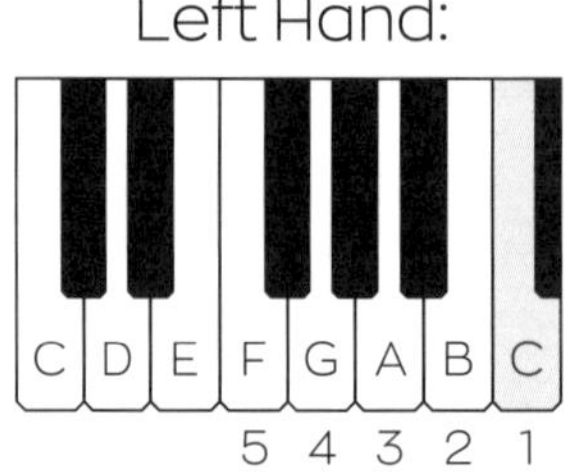

Right Hand:

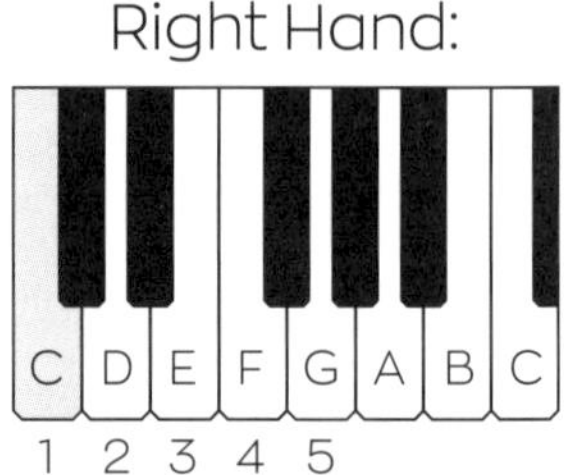

ODE TO JOY

By Ludwig van Beethoven

count: 1 2 3 4

Next, we revisit "Lean On Me." First, play through the right hand to remind yourself of the notes. Now try the left hand. This is tricky because the first three notes are all of different length. You will need to keep a careful count of the beats within the measure.

TOOLBOX

A good tip for this song is to mentally pair up the Cs and the Fs, as both hands play these two notes at the same time.

The Basics
Time Signature: 4/4 (four quarter notes per measure)
Starts on: First beat. Count, "1, 2, 3, 4," and then play.
First note: Middle C
Left Hand: The next C below middle C

LEAN ON ME

Words and Music by Bill Withers

Track 29

Note the way the left hands starts the next one and how the right hand joins in on the second beat of the measure. Remember to count yourself in.

The Basics
Time Signature: 4/4 (four quarter notes per measure)
Starts on: First beat. Count, "1, 2, 3, 4," and then play.
Right Hand: The next C above middle C
Left Hand: Middle C

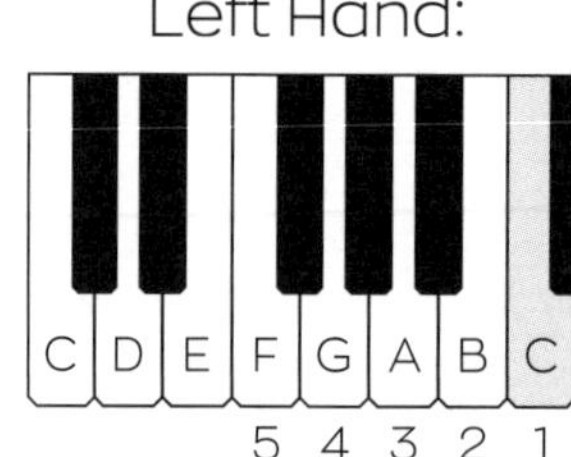

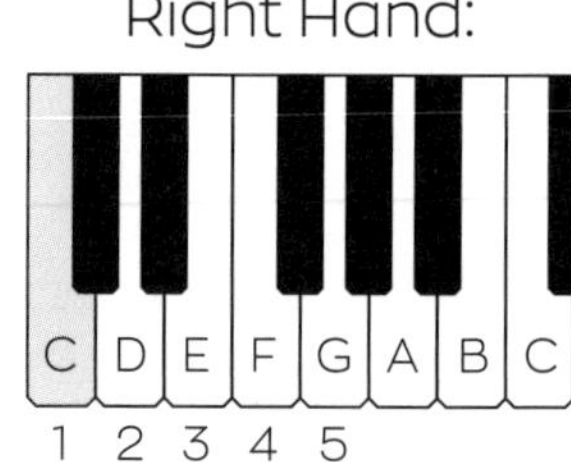

I DREAMED A DREAM

(from *Les Miserablés*)

Music by Claude-Michel Schönberg

Lyrics by Alain Boublil, Jean-Marc Natel and Herbert Kretzmer

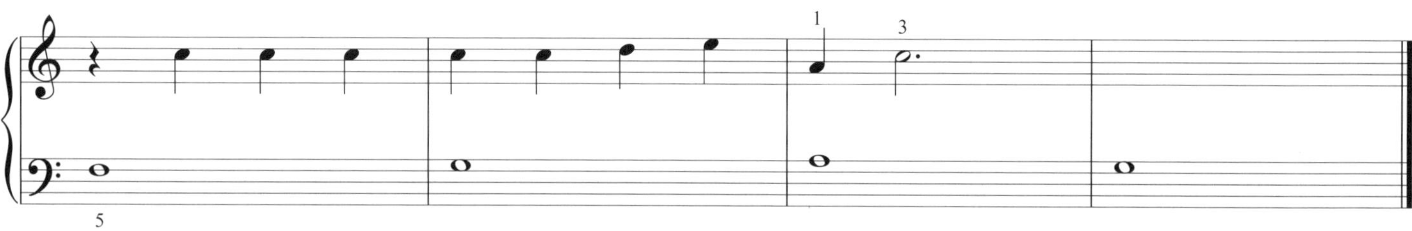

In this next song, we explore the repeat concept further. Sometimes, a song uses a repeat, but it has a different ending the second time around. In this case, the composer would use a **first time measure** (measures 16–17). Then, you repeat from the beginning. The second time through you should skip out these measures and go straight to the **second time measure**, at measure 18. This way, the song ends correctly.

There is a bit of a trap here: The right hand has to briefly move outside the five-finger position in order to play the last few notes. Just move your second finger over your thumb in the penultimate measure. Your hand will therefore move two notes down the keyboard. Try to do this as smoothly as possible. Secondly, your left hand has to stretch down to the C in measure 14; then, the thumb will be on the G in measure 16.

The Basics
Time Signature: 3/4 (three quarter notes per measure)
Starts on: First beat. Count, "1, 2, 3," and then play.
Right Hand: E above middle C
Left Hand: F below middle C

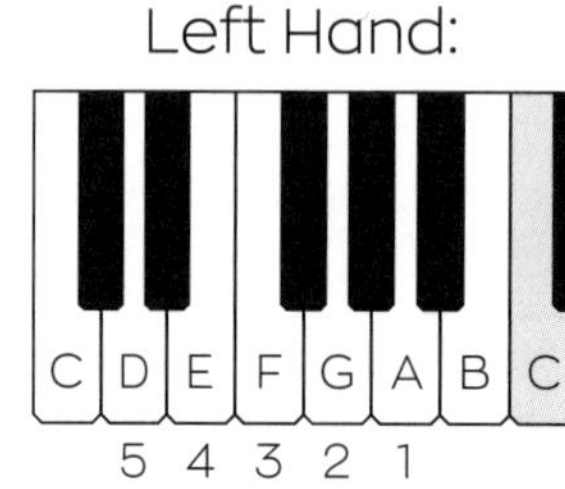

HALLELUJAH

Words and Music by Leonard Cohen

Track 30

count: 1 2 3

The Octave

Have a quick look at page 5. The distance from one C to the next is called an octave. We therefore talk of playing an octave higher or lower. In this next tune, the entire melody line is an octave higher than it was previously.

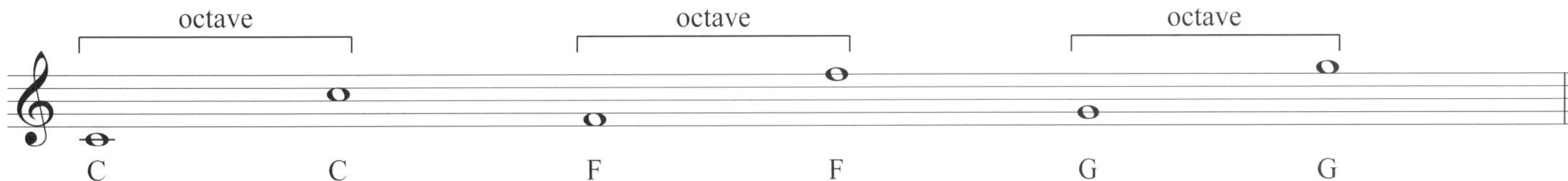

The right hand has two distinct hand positions, as indicated by the diagrams. You need to change from the first position to the second in measure 7. The left hand is more straightforward with the thumb on middle C.

The Basics
Time Signature: 4/4 (four quarter notes per measure)
Starts on: First beat. Count, "1, 2, 3, 4," and then play.
Right Hand: A above middle C
Left Hand: A below middle C

Right-Hand Position 1:

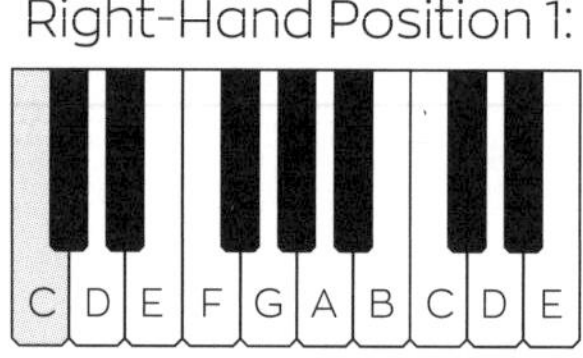

Right-Hand Position 2:

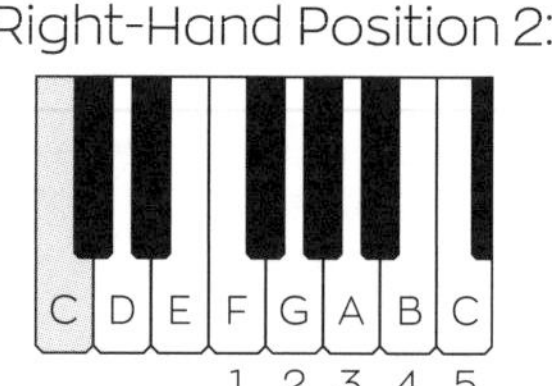

HELLO

Words and Music by Adele Adkins and Greg Kurstin

Track 31

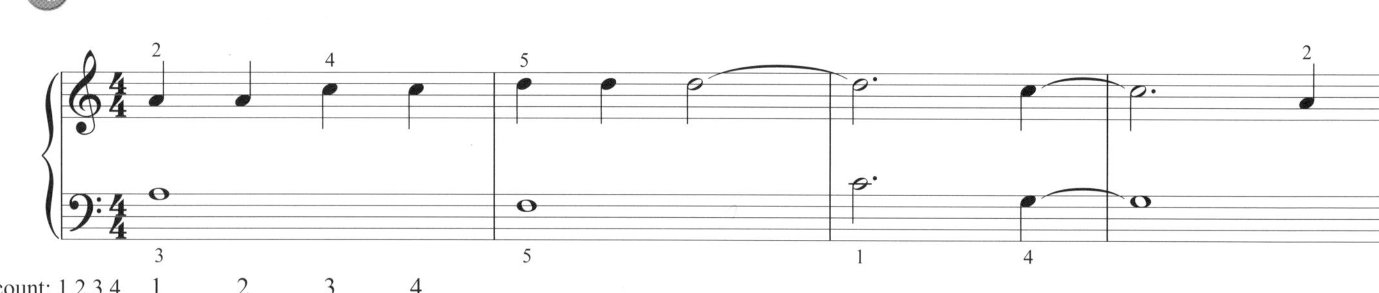

The Whole Staff

Negotiating Multiple Hand Positions

So far in the book, you have played tunes where the hands don't move beyond a single position—they're static (apart from one or two places where you need to stretch a finger down e.g., the end of "Hallelujah" on page 35). The pieces in this chapter are all about using the entire staff so that you get used to moving your hand up and down the keyboard. (This will also improve your music-reading skills.)

The folk tune "Scarborough Fair" uses two distinct hand positions. In measure 11, you need to move from the second position back to the first within a single phrase. The repeated A section helps; you can reposition your hand as you play the second A. You also have to move your thumb down a note onto middle C in measure 12.

The Basics
Time Signature: 3/4 (three quarter notes per measure)
Starts on: First beat. Count, "1, 2, 3, 4," and then play.
Right Hand: D above middle C

Position 1:

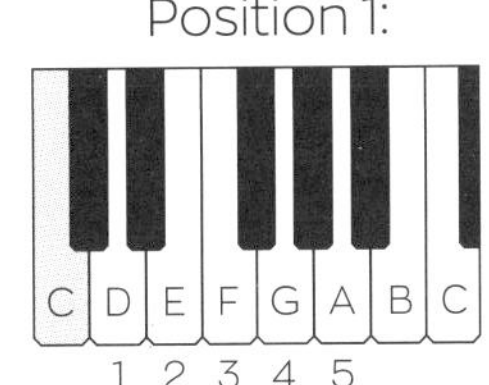

Position 2:

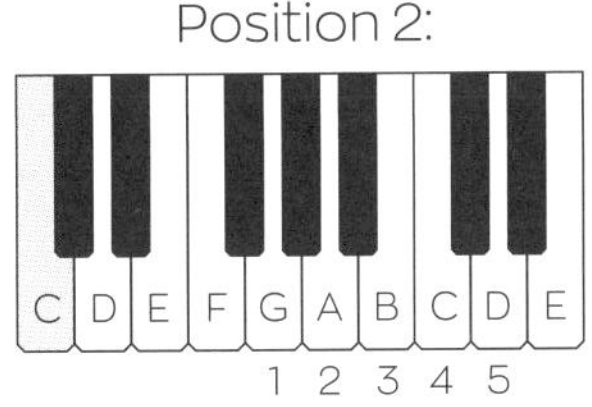

SCARBOROUGH FAIR

Traditional English

Track 32

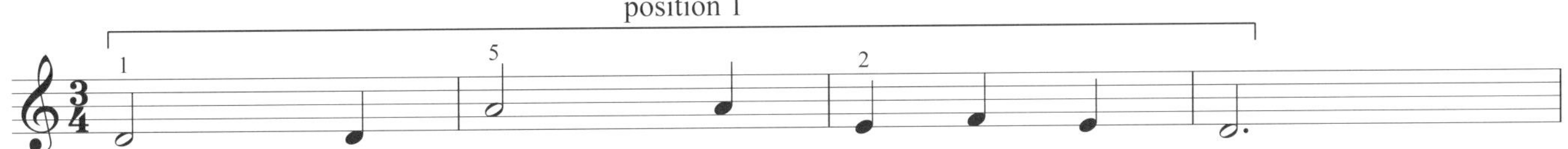

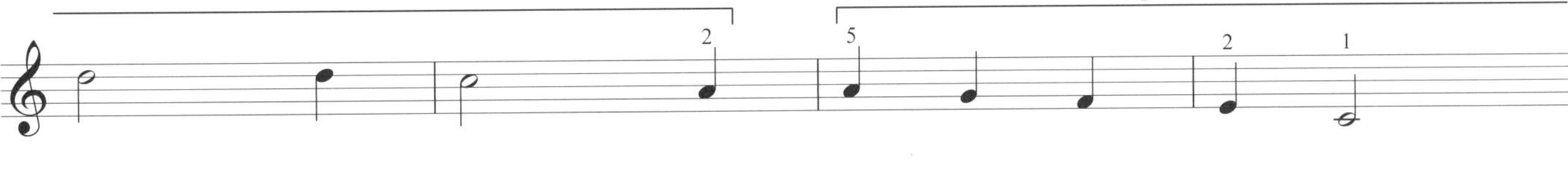

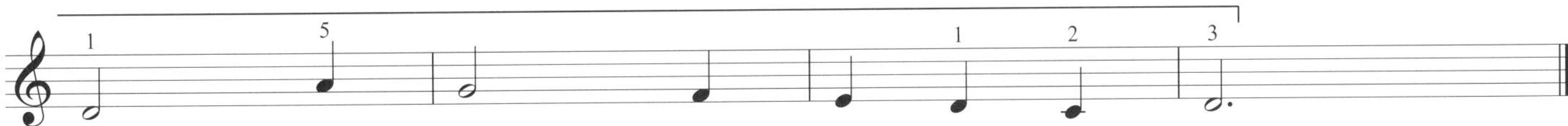

Piano Talk
In a grand piano, the frame and strings are horizontal. In an upright piano, the frame and strings are vertical.

In "When She Loved Me," you have to negotiate three different positions with the right hand. Position 2 is simply one note higher than position 1. Position 3 involves starting with the thumb lower just for the first note. So you have to keep your wits about you and follow the music carefully!

The Basics
Time Signature: 4/4 (four quarter notes per measure)
Starts on: First beat. Count, "1, 2, 3, 4," and then play.
Right Hand: G above middle C

Position 1:

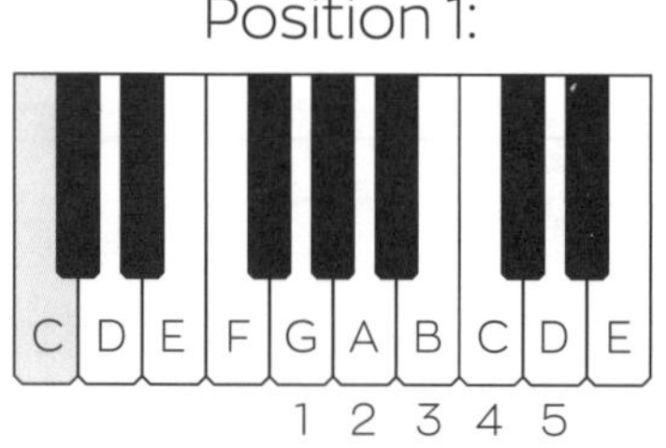

Position 2:

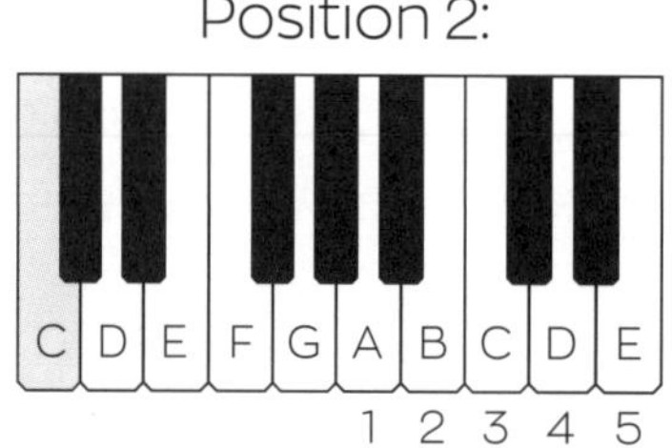

Position 3:

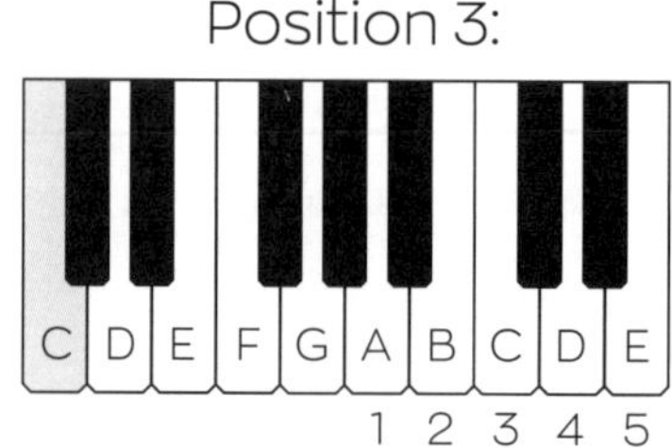

WHEN SHE LOVED ME

(from *Toy Story 2*)

Music and Lyrics by Randy Newman

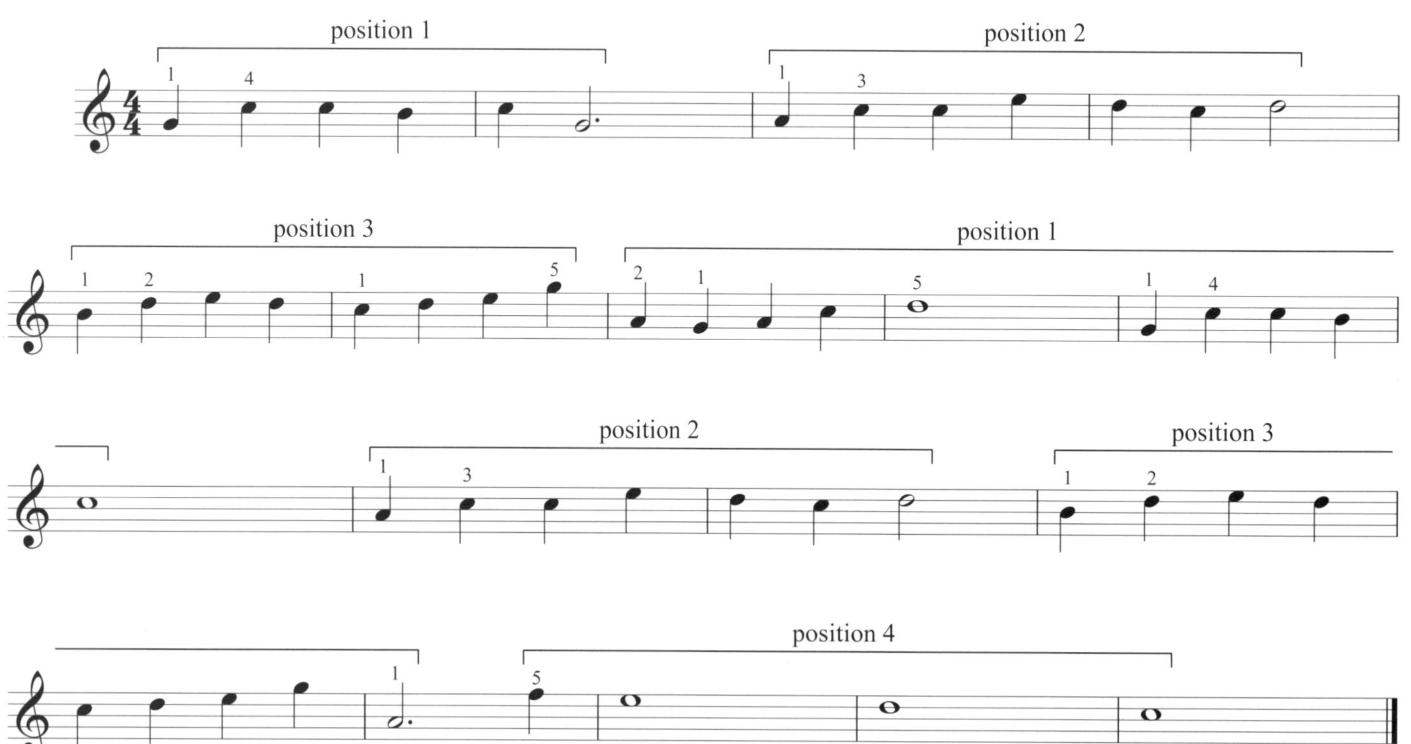

TOOLBOX

When you have more than one hand position, you will need to look ahead; you have to see the change coming while counting the beats of the measure in your head at the same time.

The next tune is a classical piece: "Can Can" by Offenbach. This is notated for the left hand, and it uses three different hand positions. Watch out: Your hand moves from one position to the next quite quickly, e.g., in the second line. This is a descending **major scale** (measures 7–9). (More on scales later.)

The Basics
Time Signature: 4/4 (four quarter notes per measure)
Starts on: First beat. Count, "1, 2, 3, 4," and then play.
Left Hand: C an octave below middle C

Position 1:

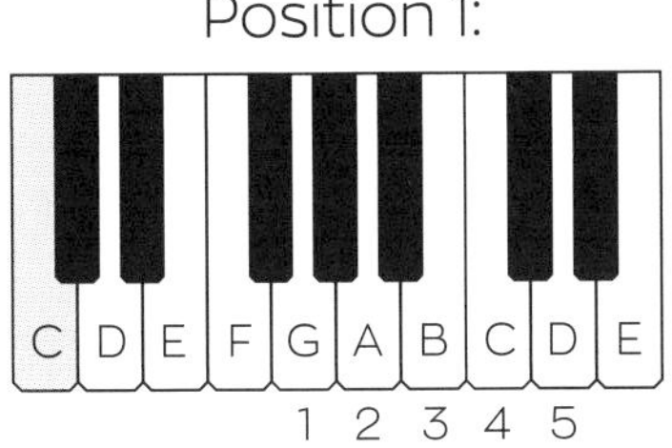

Position 2:

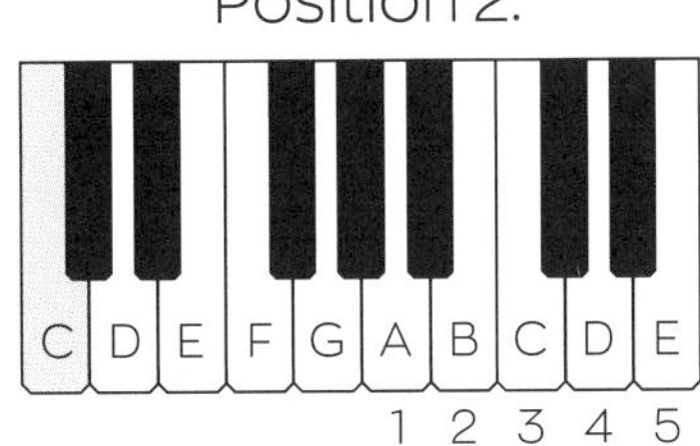

Position 3:

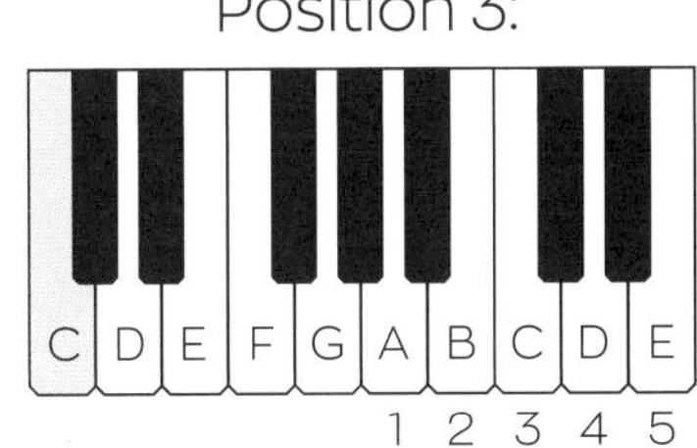

CAN CAN

(from *Orpheus in the Underworld*)

By Jacques Offenbach

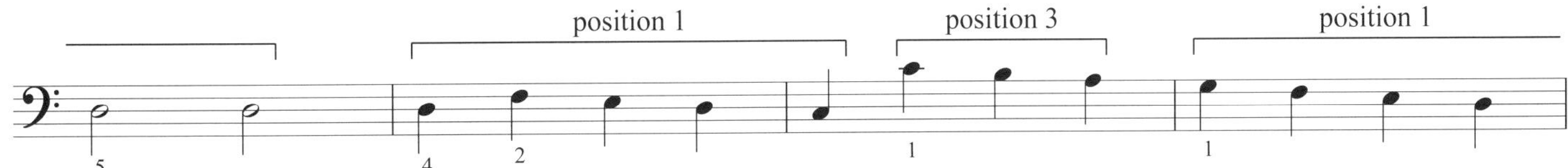

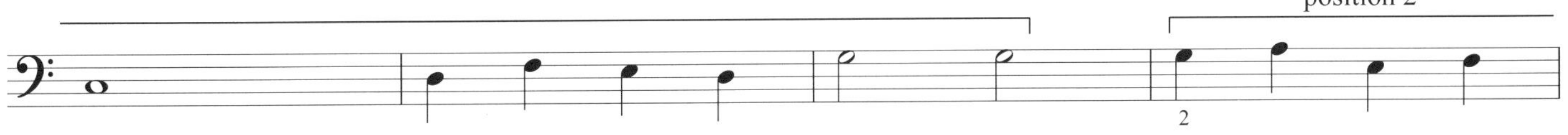

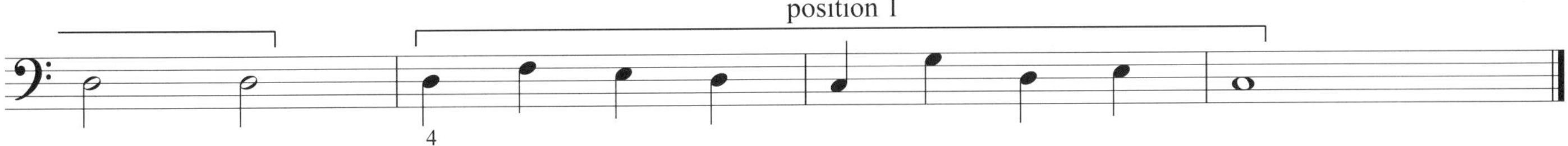

"See You Again" uses three different hand positions. A new concept here is moving from position 2 back to position 1 within a single phrase (measure 6). You must try to execute this transition carefully, counting the beats in your head as mentioned in the Toolbox. Try to keep it smooth, too. Also, note that position 1 actually involves a stretch one note outside the five-finger position.

The Basics
Time Signature: 4/4 (four quarter notes per measure)
Starts on: Second beat. Count, "3, 4, 1," and then play.
Right Hand: Middle C

Position 1:

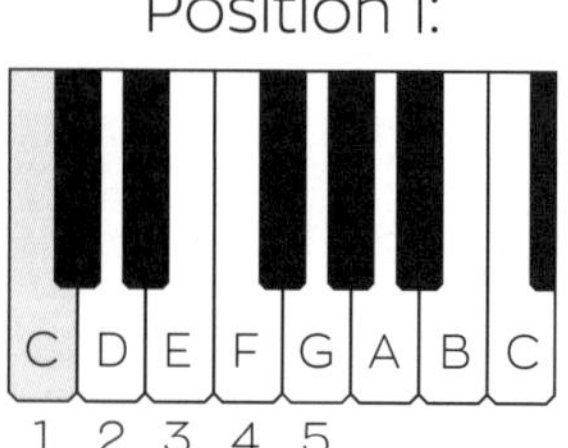

Position 2:

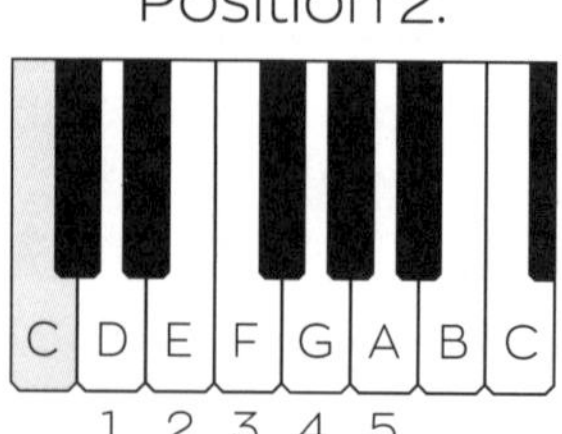

Position 3:

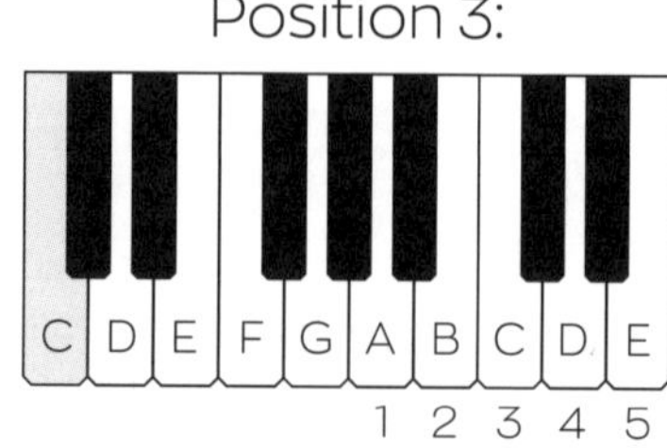

SEE YOU AGAIN

(from *Furious 7*)

Words and Music by Cameron Thomaz, Charlie Puth, Justin Franks, Andrew Cedar, Dann Hume, Josh Hardy and Phoebe Cockburn

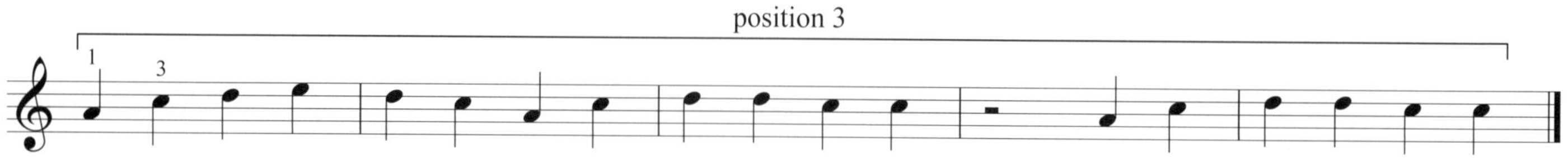

➔ Do-It-Yourself

If you want to challenge yourself further, try this:

You could try playing all these tunes with the other hand. This is similar to the DIY section on page 21, but you will need to make more complicated changes to the fingering. In "Can Can," the changes in fingering positions for the right hand will not necessarily be in the same places as they are for the left hand. Here it is printed with right-hand fingerings:

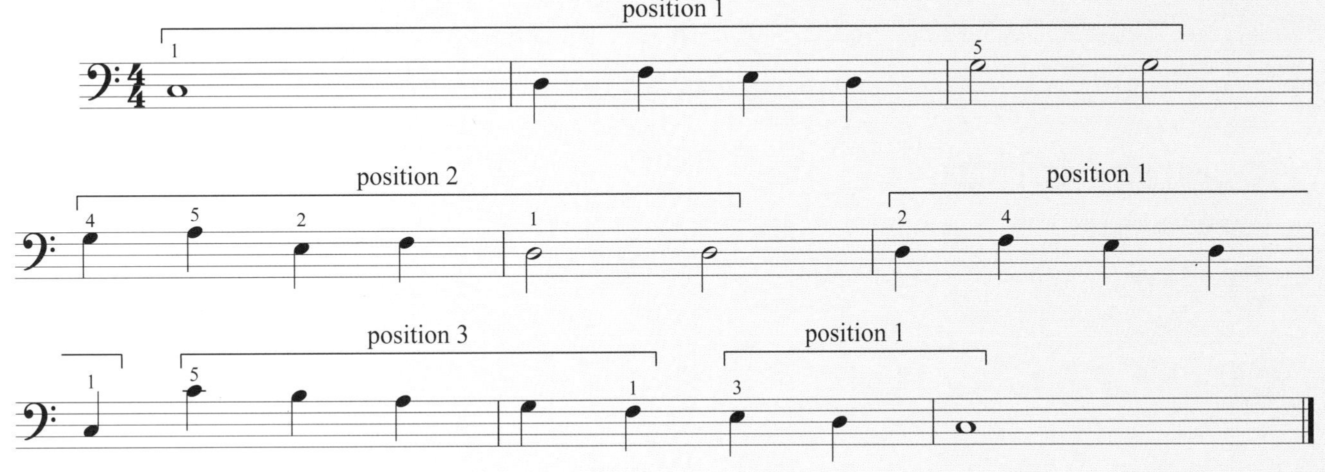

By Jacques Offenbach

So you see that because of the way the hand is shaped, the change in hand position occurs later.

Try playing the other songs with the opposite hand. You will need to try different fingerings to see what works. Write these into the music.

Technique Clinic 2

Developing an Agile Thumb

Before you play the next group of songs, it's worth trying these exercises, which are good for developing an agile thumb. If you look at the way the hand is shaped you can see there is generally more space between your thumb and forefinger than between all your other fingers. This means it is generally comfortable to play next-door notes with next door fingers, but it's good to be able to stretch the thumb out and play notes further away.

1. Rocking Motion

Keep your wrist and forearm free, especially when playing the low G with your thumb.

Track 34

Although melody lines tend to occur on the right hand, it's worth having the same degree of flexibility in the left hand. When accompanying the right hand, the left hand sometimes has to perform some acrobatics, such as octave leaps, etc.

Track 35

2. Arpeggios

Stretch out your hand over a whole octave to play this. Decide which finger you prefer to use on the third note. (More on arpeggios much later in the book.)

Track 36

R.H.:

Track 37

L.H.:

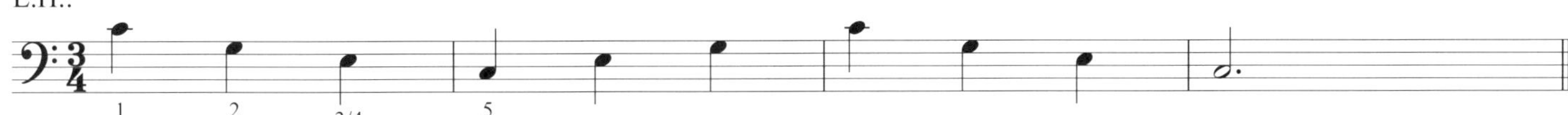

3. Spacial Awareness

Move your elbow from side to side as you play this, so that the arm movement helps the hand find the notes.

Track 38

R.H.:

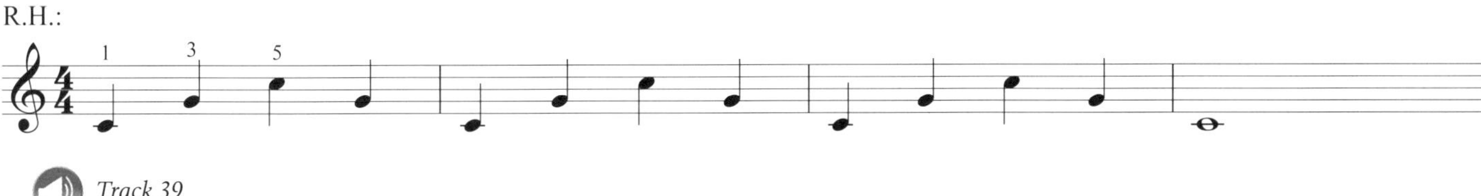

Track 39

L.H.:

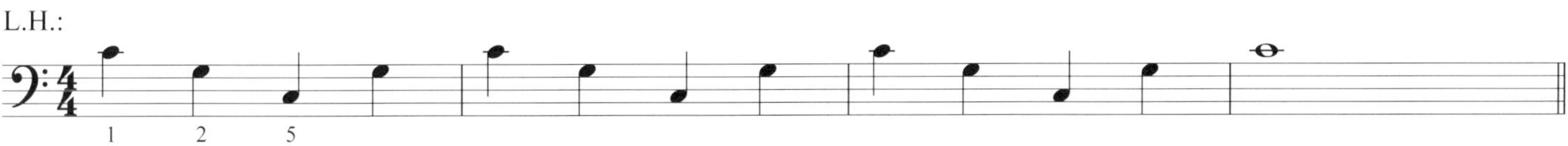

This piece ties all these ideas together. You have a big challenge towards the end: You need to stretch your right hand out and put your thumb under your fingers to get to the C at the start of measure 8. The last note is "top" C, two octaves above middle C.

WINDMILL

Track 40

Piano Talk

The largest piano ever made was by Adrian Mann, a young piano tuner from New Zealand. It is 5.7 meters long and weighs 1.4 tons. It took four years to build!

The final song in this section is "Edelweiss" from *The Sound of Music*. The melody line in this song centers on a section of notes from E up to D. Sometimes your thumb is on the E; other times, it's on the G. Similarly, your fifth finger moves from the B to the D. You have to maintain a degree of flexibility, and your hand position can change within a single phrase. Be sure to try the right hand on its own first. The left hand stays in one position throughout.

The Basics

Time Signature: 3/4 (three quarter notes per measure)

Starts on: First beat. Count, "1, 2, 3, 4," and then play.

Right Hand: E above middle C

Left Hand: C an octave below middle C

EDELWEISS

(from *The Sound of Music*)

Lyrics by Oscar Hammerstein II

Music by Richard Rodgers

Track 41

Rests

This is another important concept: the idea of the "silent beat." Music is made up of both sound and silence. We have to be able to measure the silences in the same way that we measure the sounds. Therefore, every note has its very own rest.

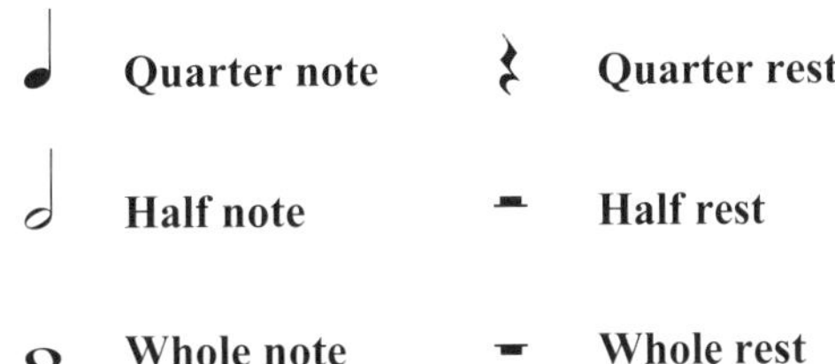

Notice the subtle difference between the half rest and the whole rest. A whole rest is also used to indicate a silent full measure, even if the piece is in 3/4.

Measures always contain the number of beats stated in the signature, but they can be either notes or rests. The following measures are all equal in length.

In this theme from *Eine Kleine Nachtmusik*, the hands must really work together. Make sure they are in the correct position before you begin with both thumbs hovering above middle C.

> **The Basics**
> **Time Signature:** 4/4 (four quarter notes per measure)
> **Starts on:** First beat. Count, "1, 2, 3, 4," and then play.
> **Left Hand:** Middle C

EINE KLEINE NACHTMUSIK, K. 525

By Wolfgang Amadeus Mozart

In the next two songs, the rests are crucial moments of silence in between phrases. If you get the counting wrong, it will sound like a hiccup. A strong sense of pulse is essential.

The Basics
Time Signature: 4/4 (four quarter notes per measure)
Starts on: First beat. Count, "1, 2, 3, 4," and then play.
Right Hand: E over an octave above middle C

HOT N COLD

Words and Music by Katy Perry, Max Martin and Lukasz Gottwald

The next song has whole measures of rest. This may seem like a lot of silent beats, but if you cut it short, it won't sound right. Once you're familiar with the notes, it might pay to play this tune a little faster.

The Basics
Time Signature: 4/4 (four quarter notes per measure)
Starts on: Third beat. Count, "1, 2," and then play.
Left Hand: E below middle C

EVERY BREATH YOU TAKE

Music and Lyrics by Sting

Each phrase in this next song starts on the third beat of a measure. You must make sure you have a really solid count of four beats going in your head as you play. Also, watch out for the tied notes.

> **The Basics**
> **Time Signature:** 4/4 (four quarter notes per measure)
> **Starts on:** Third beat. Count, "1, 2," and then play.
> **Right Hand:** Middle C

MAMMA MIA

Words and Music by Benny Andersson, Bjorn Ulvaeus and Stig Anderson

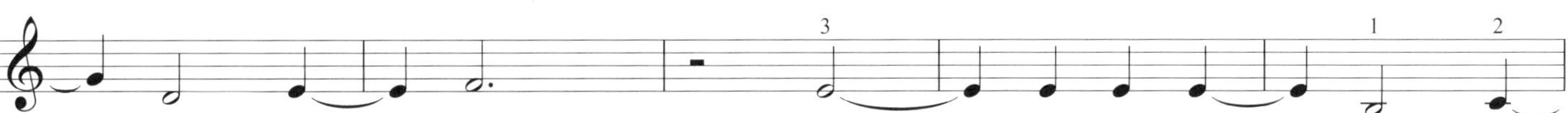

> **Piano Talk**
> The piano can play accompaniment and melody at the same time.

Finally, in this chapter, we look at a song for both hands. "Wonderwall" was a big hit for 1990s Britpop sensation Oasis. As with "Every Breath You Take," there are several whole measures of rest in the right hand. Make sure you're counting correctly. The left hand is kept very simple in this arrangement, but it has a long playout at the end.

> **The Basics**
> **Time Signature:** 4/4 (four quarter notes per measure)
> **Starts on:** First beat. Count, "1, 2, 3, 4," and then play.
> **Right Hand:** A above middle C
> **Left Hand:** D below middle C

"Wonderwall" appears on the next page to allow for easier reading.

WONDERWALL

Words and Music by Noel Gallagher

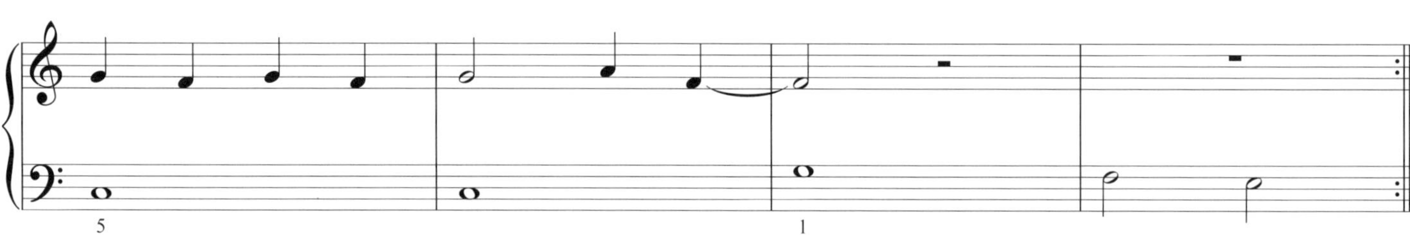

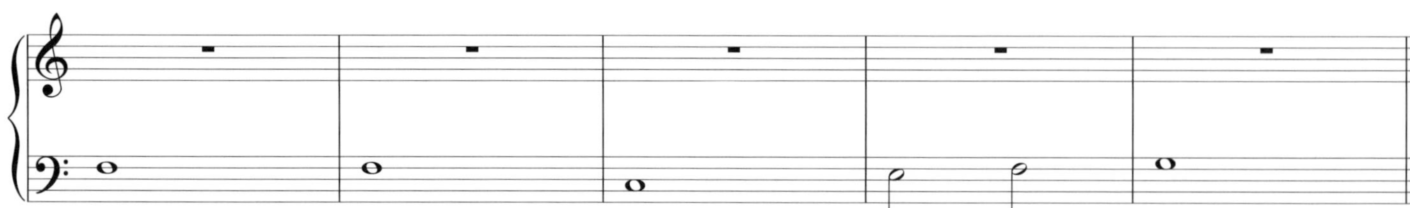

Altering the Volume

Composers use dynamics to indicate how soft or loud the music should be played. In classical music, dynamics are usually written with the symbols for the Italian words they represent. The following table lists most of the terms you will need to know.

pp	*pianissimo*	very soft
p	*piano*	soft
mp	*mezzo piano*	moderately soft
mf	*mezzo forte*	moderately loud
f	*forte*	loud
ff	*fortissimo*	very loud
<	*crescendo or cresc.*	getting gradually louder
>	*diminuendo or dim.* *or decrescendo*	getting gradually softer

Applying all these dynamic markings in order would give the following gradual crescendo:

pp <	***p*** <	***mp*** <	***mf*** <	***f*** <	***ff***
very soft	soft	moderately soft	moderately loud	loud	very loud

At the beginning of a piece of music, a single dynamic marking will usually be printed, which gives an indication of the character of the piece. Here is the main theme from the slow movement to Beethoven's *Pathetique* sonata. The dynamic marking is **piano**, so try to play this piece softly.

> **The Basics**
> **Time Signature:** 4/4 (four quarter notes per measure)
> **Starts on:** First beat. Count, "1, 2, 3, 4," and then play.
> **Right Hand:** E above middle C
> **Left Hand:** C an octave below middle C

SONATA IN C MINOR, OP. 13 'PATHÉTIQUE' (2ND MOVEMENT)

By Ludwig van Beethoven

Track 46

Whether you are playing loud or soft, you need to try to maintain an even touch at the piano so that notes don't stick out.

The next one is just for the right hand. It is to be played very loud!

> **The Basics**
> **Time Signature:** 4/4 (four quarter notes per measure)
> **Starts on:** Fourth beat. Count, "1, 2, 3," and then play.
> **Left Hand:** G above middle C

SINCE U BEEN GONE

Words and Music by Max Martin and Lukasz Gottwald

Aim for a big contrast in dynamics in the piece on the next page.

> **The Basics**
> **Time Signature:** 4/4 (four quarter notes per measure)
> **Starts on:** First beat. Count, "1, 2, 3, 4," and then play.
> **Left Hand:** E over an octave above middle C

CAN CAN

(from *Orpheus in the Underworld*)

By Jacques Offenbach

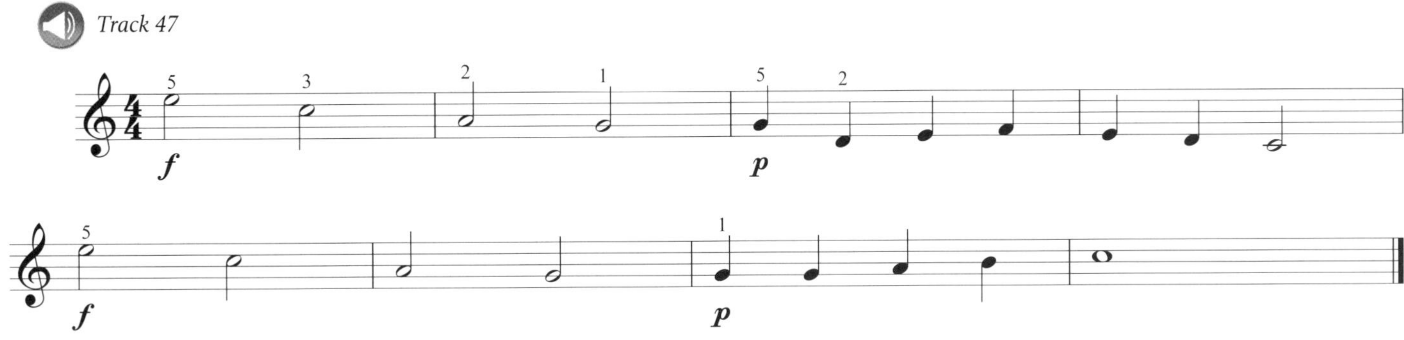

Smooth versus Detached Playing

Articulation refers to the way you physically approach playing notes on the piano: the onset of a note (sometimes called the "attack") and its duration. As well as observing notes values to determine length, the articulation can be indicated by curved lines and dots.

The Slur

Let's take two different notes: If we put a curved line over the top of them, it indicates that they should be played smoothly, without a gap in between. In this example, you would lean slightly on the third finger and lighten your touch on the second finger. Make sure there is no gap between them.

Legato

Legato is the proper Italian term for smooth playing.

Remember to lean slightly on the first note of each slur.

Tie or Slur: What's the Difference?

At first glance, there is no difference; they both look the same. The rule is this: If the two notes are the same, it's a tie, and if they're different, it's a slur.

Slur: Play these two notes smoothly

Tie: Join these two notes together

Notice the way this next song is actually a series of slurs—short phrases of notes that belong together. As you re-articulate the C, there will naturally be a small gap beforehand, but there should be no gaps between notes under the slurs.

> **The Basics**
> **Time Signature:** 4/4 (four quarter notes per measure)
> **Starts on:** First beat. Count, "1, 2, 3, 4," and then play.
> **Left Hand:** C an octave below middle C

LEAN ON ME

Words and Music by Bill Withers

Track 49

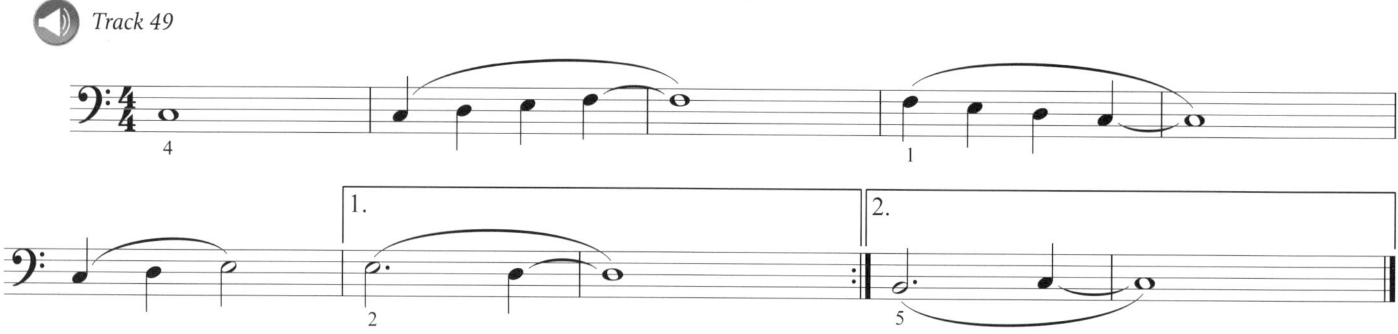

Staccato

Staccato is the opposite of legato: short and detached. It is indicated by a dot placed directly below the note head (or above if the stem is coming down). Play with a loose wrist, like you're bouncing a ball.

THE SURPRISE SYMPHONY

By Franz Joseph Haydn

Track 50

> **Piano Talk**
> The word **piano** is the shortened version of the word **pianoforte** because of its ability to play notes both quietly (piano) and loudly (forte). The harpsichords that came before could only play quietly.

Now we'll look at a longer piece: an extract from *Beauty and the Beast*. This involves everything you have learned so far at the piano: playing a mixture of different note values, several hand positions in the right hand, playing hands together, and playing with dynamics. Note the phrasing: Each group of two measures is slurred together to reflect the way it would be sung. Try to play these phrases as smoothly as you can. Be careful with the structure—the song has a repeat, with first- and second-time measures. Familiarize yourself with the geography of the song before playing.

The Basics
Time Signature: 4/4 (four quarter notes per measure)
Starts on: First beat. Count, "1, 2, 3, 4," and then play.
Right Hand: E above middle C
Left Hand: C an octave below middle C

BEAUTY AND THE BEAST

(from *Beauty and the Beast*)

Music by Alan Menken
Lyrics by Howard Ashman

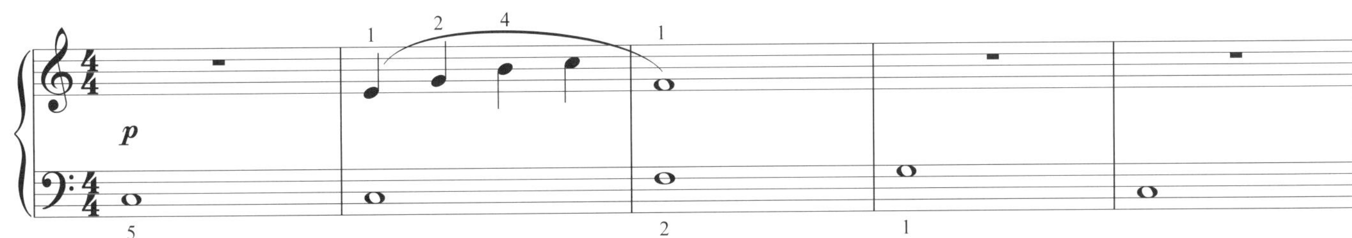

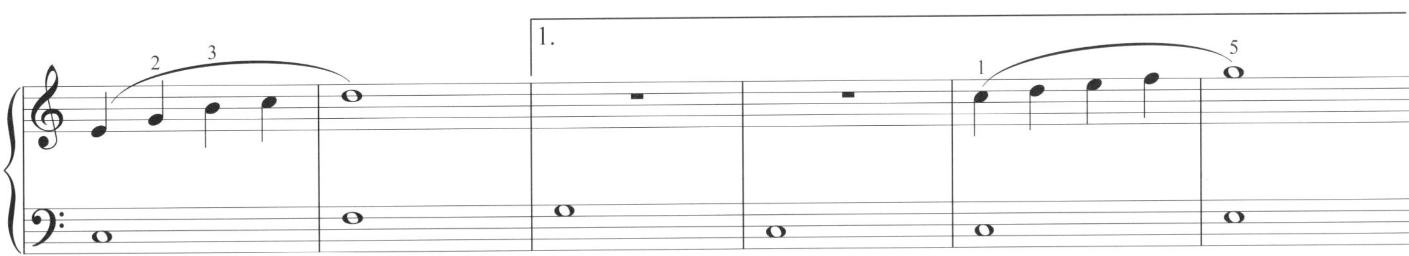

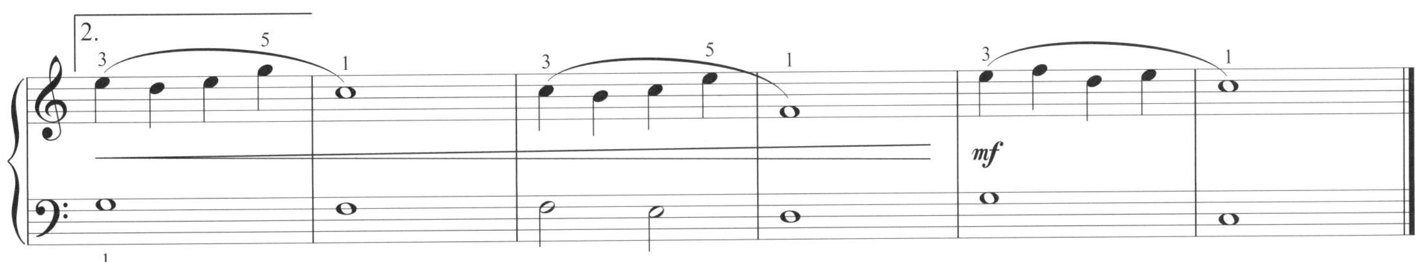

➔ Do-It-Yourself
Now go back over previous sections of the book and add some dynamic markings to any of the songs you like e.g., "Mamma Mia" on page 47 could be ***pp*** at the beginning and ***mf*** at measure 9.

Technique Clinic 3

Contrasts

The exercises in this clinic involve a small group of notes but in a wide variety of dynamics and articulation. This is so you get used to varying your touch at the instrument. You must really listen carefully to your playing here.

1. Soft/Loud/Smooth/Detached

Four different ways of playing the same sequence of notes. The left hand must imitate the right hand exactly. Remember to keep your wrists relaxed when playing loud.

Track 52

2. Crescendo/Diminuendo

On the next page, see if you can really grade your crescendo gradually over the three measures, so that you don't peak too soon. Now try it the other way around.

Track 53

Track 54

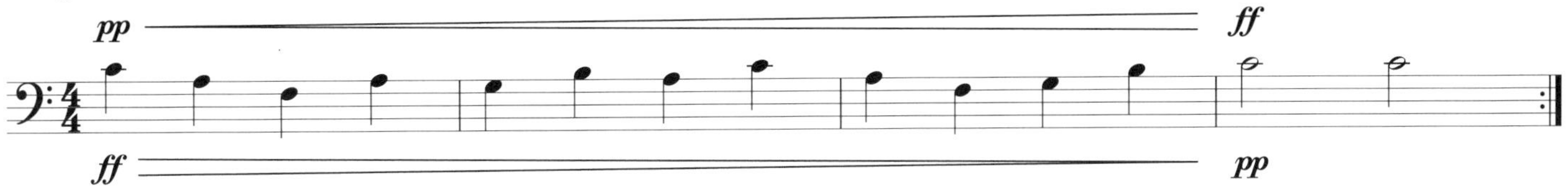

BIG DIFFERENCE

Track 55

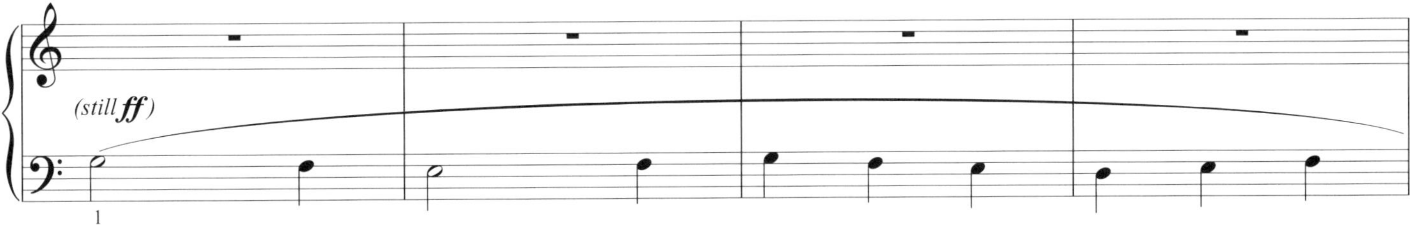

Eighth and 16th Notes

Dividing Up the Beat

So far, you've thought of a quarter note as being the base upon which all your counting is built. But it's possible to divide the beat in half, so that we get two eighth notes on every beat instead of one quarter note. And we can divide it in half again, so that we get four 16th notes in place of a quarter note.

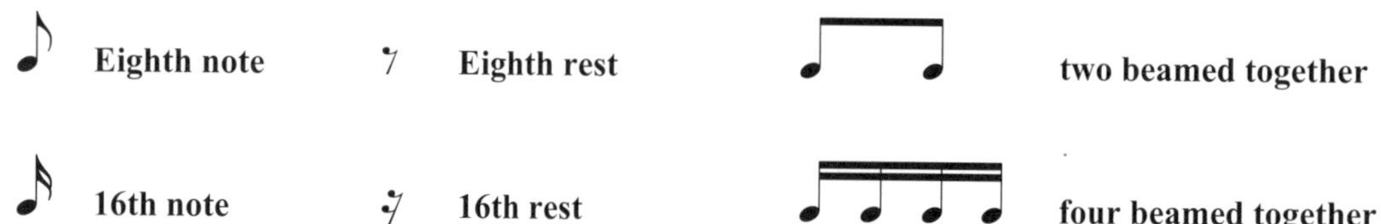

The third column above shows the number of notes needed to make a full, quarter-note beat. Remember that measures can be made up of any combination of different note values, so long as the total number of beats adds up to the number stated in the time signature. The following measures are all equal in length.

Try playing these measures through, on any note, just to practice hearing/feeling these rhythms. It's worth counting, "1 and 2 and 3 and 4 and," in your head as you play, as this subdivides the beat neatly in half.

Before playing the next tune, try the following exercise as a warm-up:

The Basics
Time Signature: 4/4 (four quarter notes per measure)
Starts on: Fourth beat. Count, "1, 2, 3," and then play.
Right Hand: G above middle C

WILLIAM TELL OVERTURE

By Giachino Rossini

Track 59

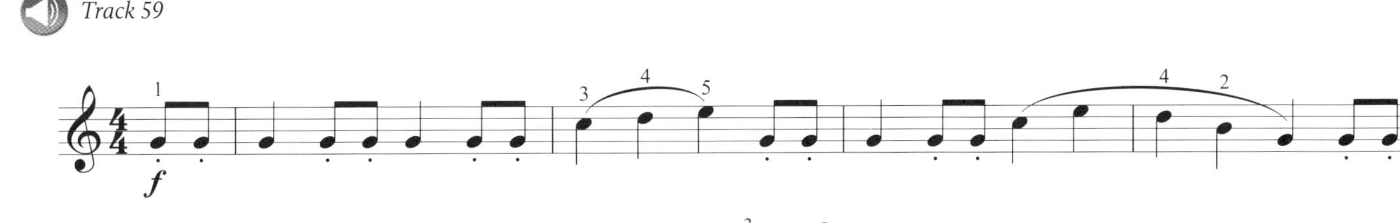

Now we'll try the same piece again, but this time it is written in eighth and 16th notes. We have simply halved all the note values, so it should sound exactly the same as the above tune. There is also a left-hand accompaniment this time.

Track 60

"Colors of the Wind" starts halfway through the fourth beat, so you must count yourself in carefully in this song.

The Basics
Time Signature: 4/4 (four quarter notes per measure)
Starts on: Second half of fourth beat. Count, "1, 2, 3, 4," and then play.
Right Hand: G above middle C
Left Hand: C an octave below middle C

COLORS OF THE WIND

(from *Pocahontas*)

Music by Alan Menken

Lyrics by Stephen Schwartz

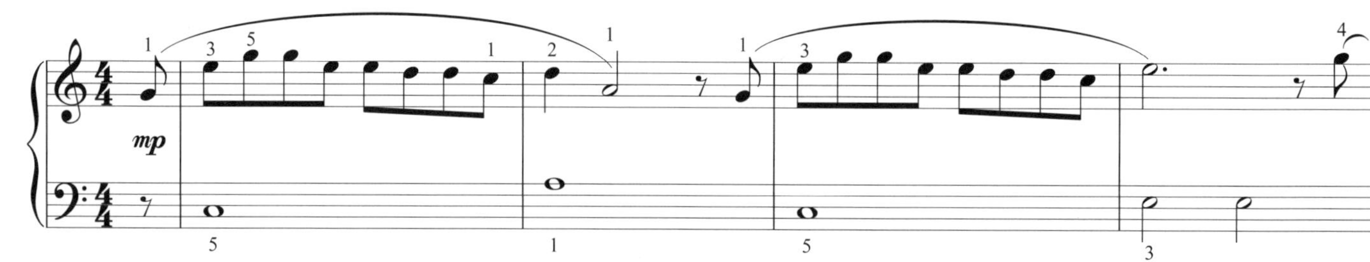

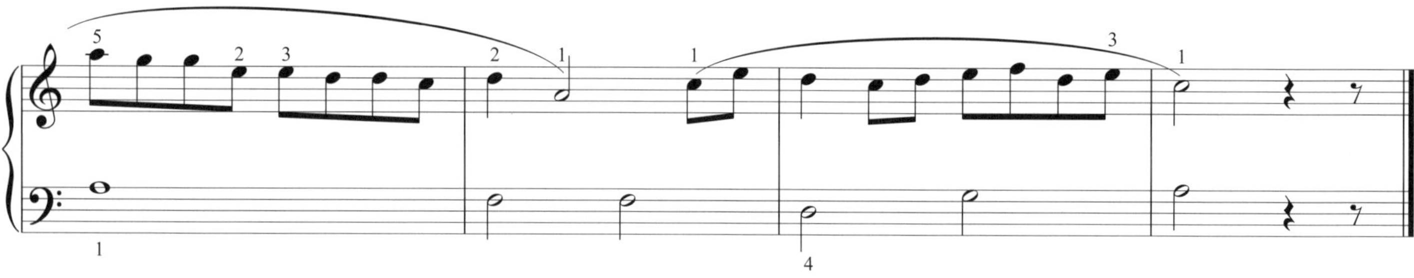

Ledger Lines

The first note in measure 5 is a top A. It is on its own line above the staff, like middle C. This is called a **ledger line**. Ledger lines enable the system of lines and spaces to continue in both directions—above and below the staff.

You will immediately see that the notes below middle C on the treble clef are exactly the same notes as the ones at the top of the bass clef staff, like this:

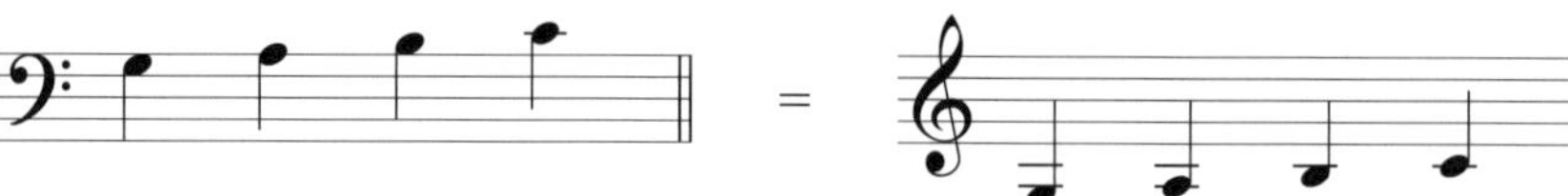

The reason you may see one instead of the other depends on the context of the music. It may be that a melody starts off higher in the treble clef, but then dips down below the staff just for one or two notes.

Here's a well-known Christmas carol. Notice how the left hand actually plays the beginning of the tune but then passes it over to the right hand. Try and keep this legato—no gap between the G and the C. Be careful in the second line as the tune passes to the left hand for one note only, then back to the right hand. The same thing happens at the end. Try to make these transitions as smooth as possible, without any bumps.

Note the various different hand positions required: The right hand in particular keeps changing position, so you will have to keep your wits about you. The most important thing is maintaining a legato touch throughout.

The Basics
Time Signature: 3/4 (three quarter notes per measure)
Starts on: Third beat. Count, "1, 2," and then play.
Right Hand: Middle C
Left Hand: G below middle C

AWAY IN A MANGER (THE CRADLE SONG)

Traditional Carol
Words by John T. McFarland (v.3)
Music by William J. Kirkpatrick

In the next song, the right hand is rather busy in the chorus, with lots of eighth notes. Be careful to stay in time with all the repeated Ds. You need to keep the left-hand half notes firm.

The Basics
Time Signature: 4/4 (four quarter notes per measure)
Starts on: Second beat. Count, "3, 4, 1," and then play.
Right Hand: E over an octave above middle C
Left Hand: D below middle C

SHAKE IT OFF

Words and Music by Taylor Swift, Max Martin and Shellback

Track 62

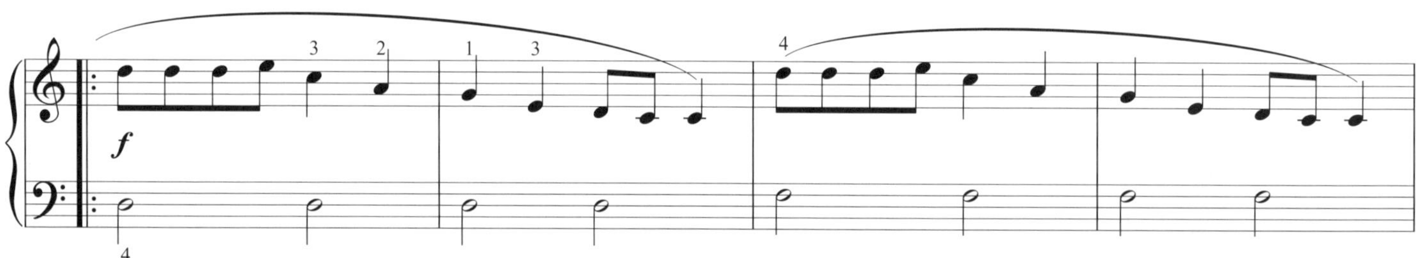

We finish this section with an arrangement of the well-known "Flower Duet," which is from an opera. Try to keep the right-hand eighth notes in measures 5–7 smooth.

The Basics

Time Signature: 3/4 (three quarter notes per measure)

Starts on: First beat. Count, "1, 2, 3," and then play.

Right Hand: E over an octave above middle C

Left Hand: C an octave below middle C

FLOWER DUET

(from *Lakmé*)

By Leo Delibes

Track 63

Introducing the Black Keys

Whole Steps and Half Steps

So far, you've learned a lot just using the white keys of the piano. It's time to learn about the black keys.

A **half step** is the smallest distance on the piano. If you start on middle C and play every single note going up, you will play a mixture of white and black keys. Each **interval** is a half step. This is also called a **semitone**.

A **whole step** = two half steps. If you start on F and play the white keys going up to the right, each interval is a whole step. This is also called a **tone**.

Half Steps

Whole Steps

Sharps and Flats

There are important symbols that indicate when to play the black keys:

If the **sharp** sign (♯) is placed immediately before a note, you must play the note a half step higher (to the right).

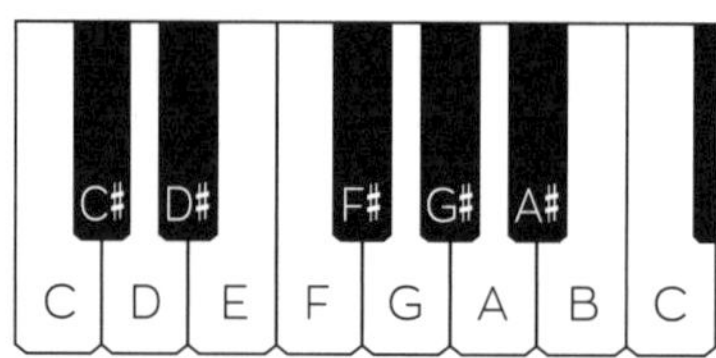

Practice finding sharps up and down the keyboard.

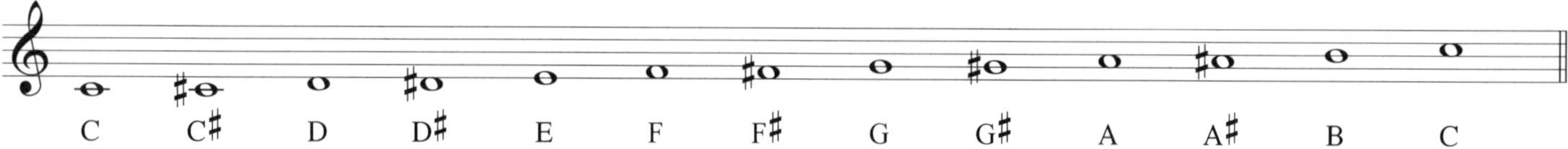

If the **flat** sign (♭) is placed immediately before a note, you must play the note a half step lower (to the left).

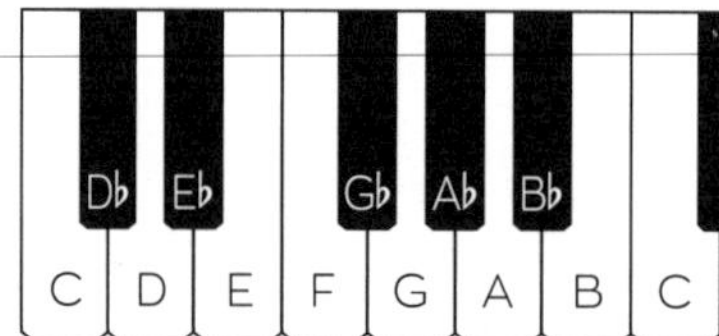

Practice finding flats up and down the keyboard.

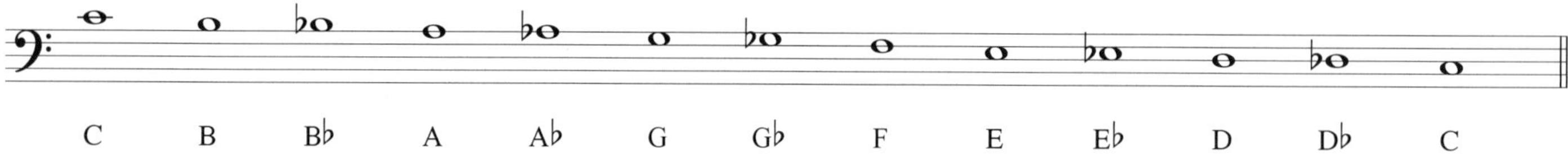

You will then notice that all black keys can have two possible names. An F♯ is exactly the same note as a G♭. The context of the music will determine which is used.

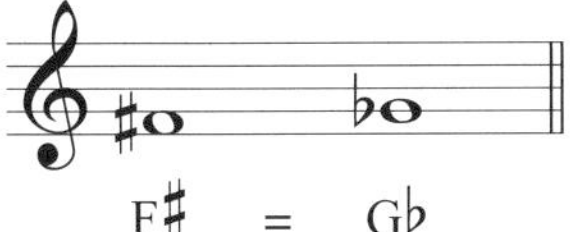

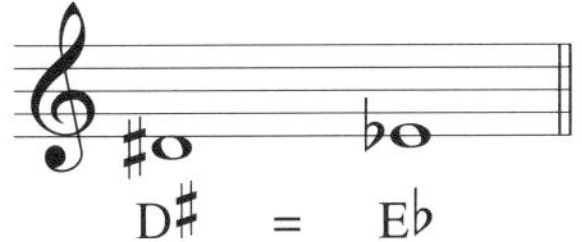

The following short extracts from pop tunes all use sharps or flats.

This tune involves an F♯. Note the slightly unusual fingering in this one; the second finger has to move over the thumb.

WE FOUND LOVE

Words and Music by Calvin Harris

An important point to note: When a sharp or flat (commonly called an **accidental**) is present in a measure, it is valid for the whole measure i.e., we don't need a sharp sign in front of the next note on that line or space.

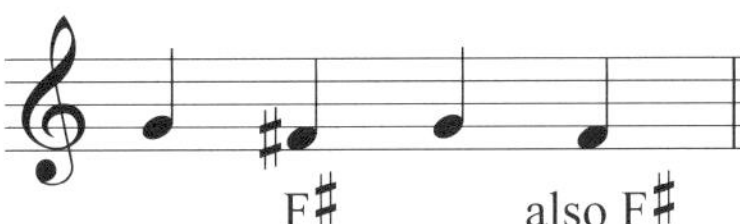

The next one has a C♯. The second note here is also C♯.

PARTY ROCK ANTHEM

Words and Music by David Listenbee, Stefan Gordy, Skyler Gordy and Peter Schroeder

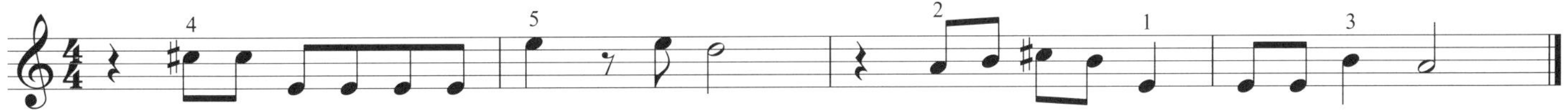

The Natural

If we have a sharp and then want the "ordinary" note to follow, we need to use the **natural** sign (♮).

So in the above example, if we wanted an ordinary F to follow the F♯, we would need to use the natural sign:

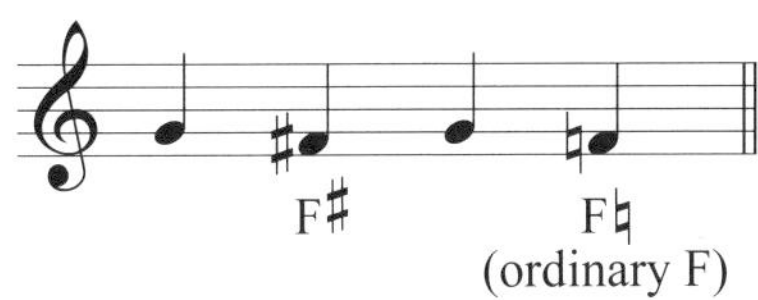

This next song has an F♯ in the second measure, but two notes later there's an F♮. The last measure has two E♭s. Careful with the rhythm—there are 16th notes as well as eighth notes.

The final extract also makes use of the natural sign. The second D♯ requires a fresh sharp sign (due to the bar line) but the next time D appears, the natural cancels out the sharp.

FÜR ELISE, WOO 59

By Ludwig van Beethoven

Track 64

A longer version of this piece appears on page 110.

Now we look at three short extracts from Beatles songs, each involving some black notes. In the first song, the left hand has an F♯ in measure 4, but this is followed by F♮ in measure 5. You have several half steps here, so you need to contract your hand a little.

The Basics
Time Signature: 3/4 (three quarter notes per measure)
Starts on: First beat. Count, "1, 2, 3," and then play.
Right Hand: C♯ an octave and a half step above middle C
Left Hand: A below middle C

LUCY IN THE SKY WITH DIAMONDS

Words and Music by John Lennon and Paul McCartney

The next song has more notes for the left hand. There are also several hand positions for the right hand.

The Basics
Time Signature: 4/4 (four quarter notes per measure)
Starts on: First beat. Count, "1, 2, 3, 4," and then play.
Right Hand: G above middle C
Left Hand: F below middle C

YESTERDAY

Words and Music by John Lennon and Paul McCartney

Track 65

The final song in this section is a little trickier for the right hand. Be careful with the rhythm in measure 5. It would help to give the song a quick listen first.

The Basics
Time Signature: 4/4 (four quarter notes per measure)
Starts on: Fourth beat. Count, "1, 2, 3," and then play.
Right Hand: A above middle C
Left Hand: D below middle C

HEY JUDE

Words and Music by John Lennon and Paul McCartney

Track 66

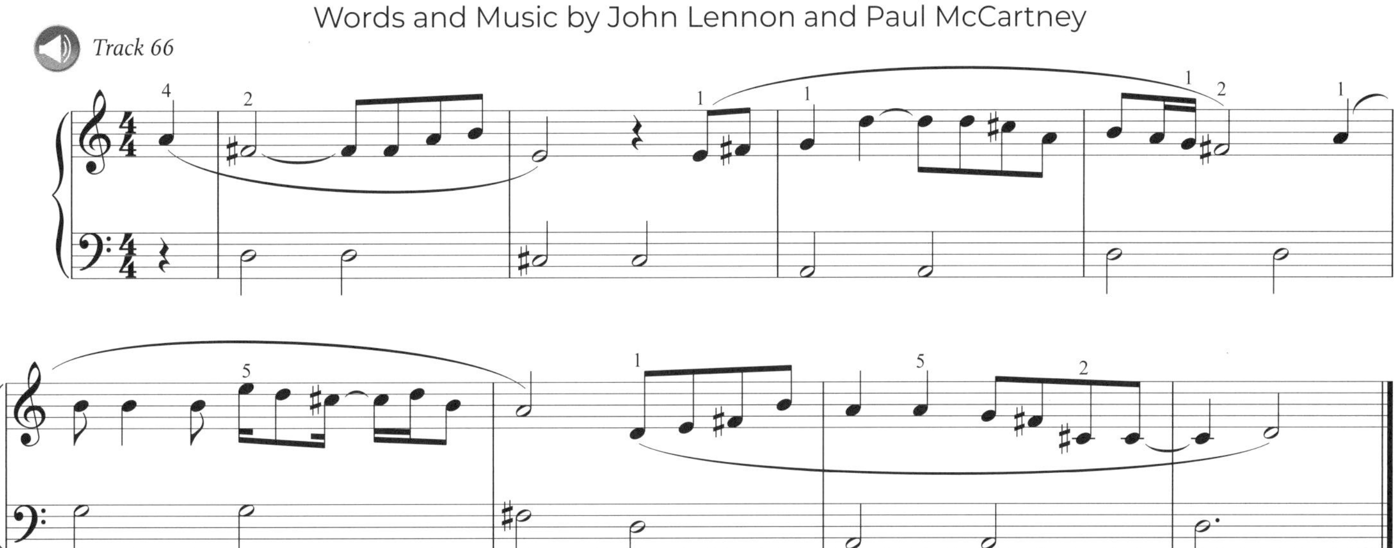

Piano Talk
There are 18 million non-professional piano players in the US alone!

The next piece is by the 20th century Hungarian composer Béla Bartók. Here, both hands stay in one position throughout, with the left hand playing the only two black notes in the piece: F♯ and G♯.

TOOLBOX

When you have sharps and flats to play, you should position your hand so that your fingers are sitting above those notes right from the beginning of the phrase.

The Basics
Time Signature: 3/4 (three quarter notes per measure)
Starts on: First beat. Count, "1, 2, 3," and then play.
Right Hand: A above middle C

DIALOGUE I

(from *The First Term at the Piano*)
By Béla Bartók
Edited by Richard Walters

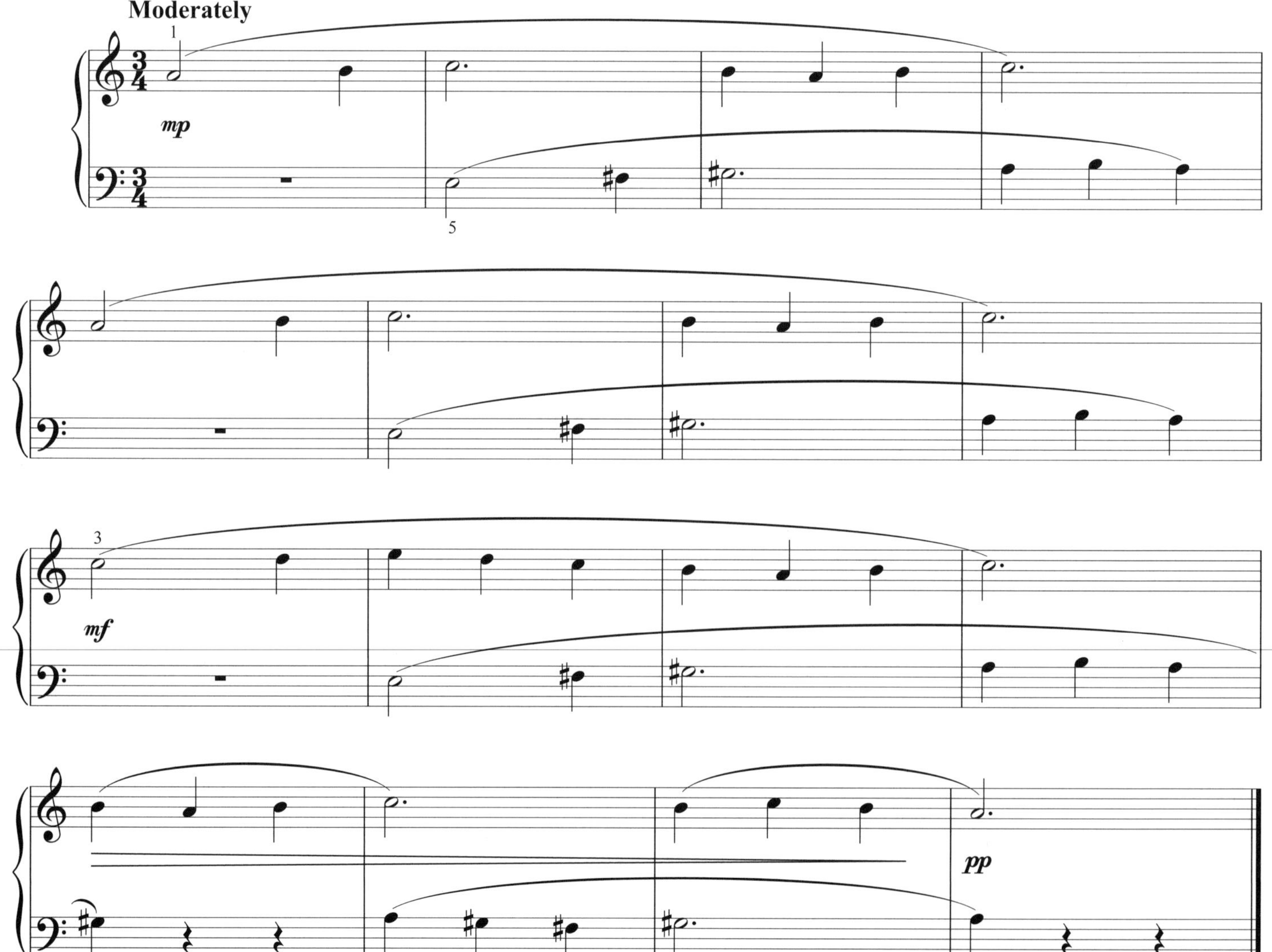

And here's "The Bare Necessities" from *The Jungle Book*. Here the left hand plays punchy quarter notes, mainly at the start of each measure. This gives the song a real sense of drive.

The Basics
Time Signature: 4/4 (four quarter notes per measure)
Starts on: Second beat. Count, "3, 4, 1," and then play.
Right Hand: Middle C
Left Hand: F below middle C

THE BARE NECESSITIES

(from *The Jungle Book*)

Words and Music by Terry Gilkyson

Dotted Rhythms

("Deck the Hall" appears on page 71.)

You have already met the **dotted half note**. This is worth three beats, as opposed to a normal half note which is worth two. A **dot**, therefore, increases a note's value by half. A dotted quarter note is worth one and a half beats, and a dotted whole note is worth six.

Look at the following note value relationships:

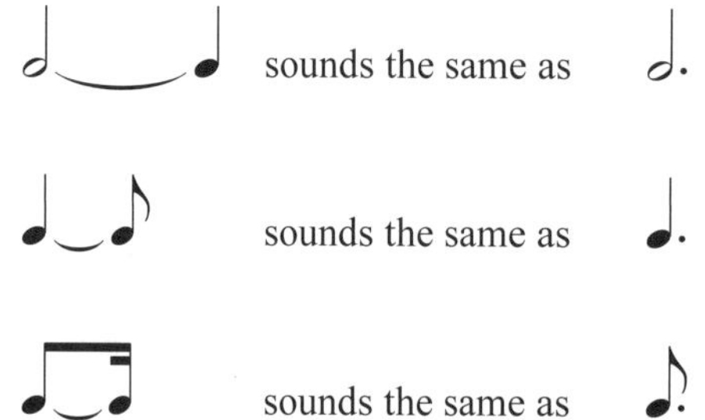

If a tie or a dot has been used, this usually means there is a short note left over. For example, a dotted quarter note is usually followed by an eighth note, so that the math adds up properly. This is then referred to as a **dotted rhythm**.

In the following example, you don't play on the beats in parentheses; you just hold the dotted notes.

Track 67

TOOLBOX

A strong sense of pulse is necessary when negotiating dotted rhythms because you have to *feel* a beat of the measure without playing a note on it.

GREENSLEEVES

Sixteenth Century Traditional English

Track 68

LA DONNA E MOBILE

(from *Rigoletto*)

By Giuseppe Verdi

Track 69

YELLOW SUBMARINE

Words and Music by John Lennon and Paul McCartney

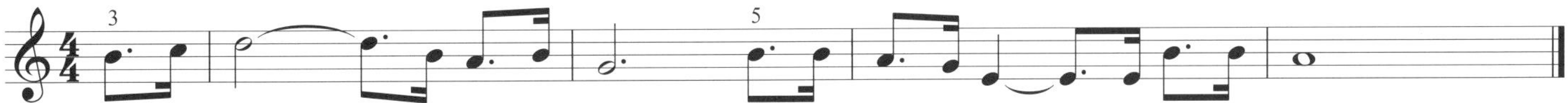

I'VE GOT MY EYE ON YOU

(from *Pirates of the Caribbean: Dead Man's Chest*)

Music by Hans Zimmer

The Basics
Time Signature: 4/4 (four quarter notes per measure)
Starts on: First beat. Count, "1, 2, 3, 4," and then play.
Right Hand: E above Middle C
Left Hand: C an octave below Middle C

NEW WORLD SYMPHONY (THEME)

By Antonín Dvořák

Track 70

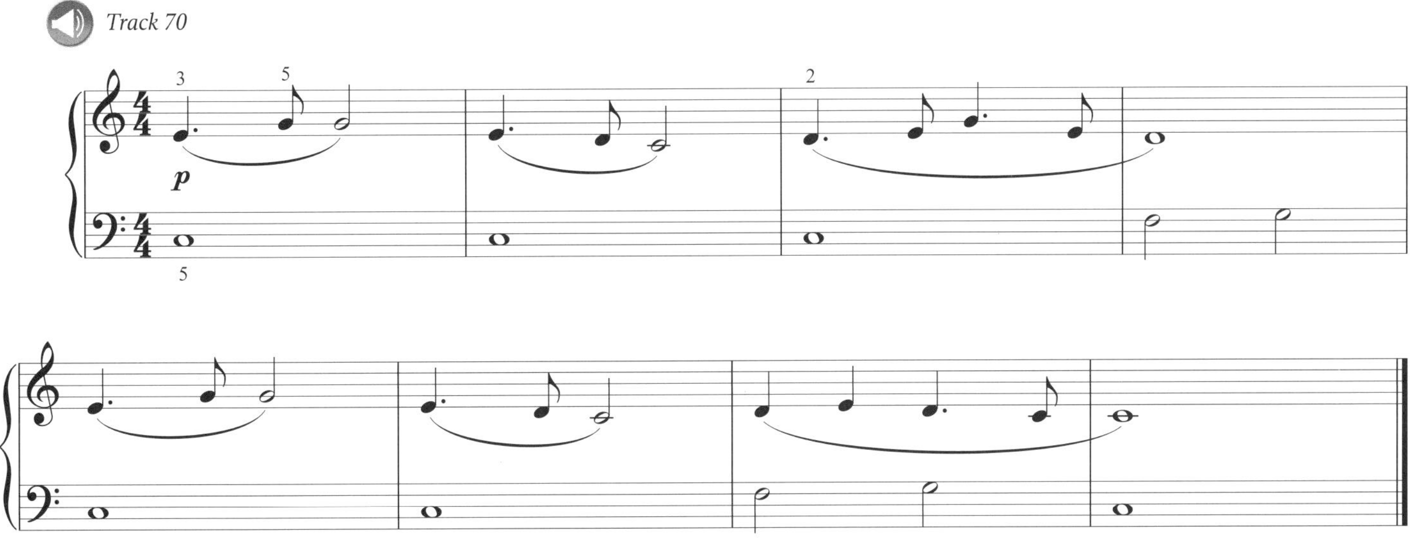

The next piece is an extract from an opera **aria** (song). The right hand has several dotted rhythms, while the left hand just plays staccato notes on the first and third beat of every measure.

The Basics
Time Signature: 4/4 (four quarter notes per measure)
Starts on: First beat. Count, "1, 2, 3, 4," and then play.
Right Hand: D over an octave above middle C
Left Hand: G below middle C

TOREADOR SONG

(from *Carmen*)

By Georges Bizet

Track 71

The next one is a well-known Christmas carol. This features frequent dotted rhythms in the right hand. Watch out for sharps; there are several F♯s and a C♯ in measure 7.

The Basics
Time Signature: 4/4 (four quarter notes per measure)
Starts on: First beat. Count, "1, 2, 3, 4," and then play.
Right Hand: D over an octave above middle C
Left Hand: G over an octave below middle C

DECK THE HALL

Traditional Welsh Carol

Track 72

Piano Talk
The piano has the widest range of all instruments—lower than the bassoon and higher than the piccolo. This is an entire orchestral range in one instrument!

Now we'll tackle something longer. "Skyfall" by Adele has examples of dotted half notes, dotted quarter notes and dotted eighth notes. The dotted rhythm of the chorus is tricky because the 16th note is tied to a half note. It would help if you give the song a quick listen.

Drills

The left hand features the famous "James Bond" riff, which you will hear in many songs. This involves a stretch beyond the five-finger position and both B♭ and B♮. It's worth practicing on its own.

Track 73

The right hand has several dotted rhythms in this song. The most difficult passage is measure 12 where you have to subdivide beat 3 to accommodate a 16th note and a dotted eighth note. This is a dotted rhythm that works the other way around: a short note followed by a long note. In order to do this, you need to divide the beat into four equal parts, and the notes you play are on the first two.

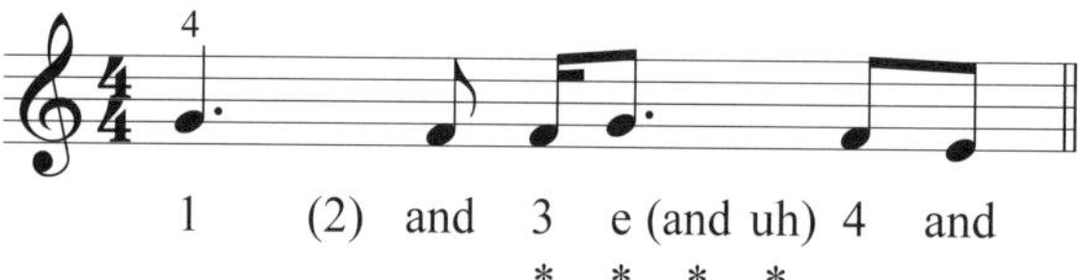

This song also introduces a chord at the end—notice that you have to play several notes at once? Try to aim for all notes to sound exactly together. (More on chords later in the book.)

> **The Basics**
> **Time Signature:** 4/4 (four quarter notes per measure)
> **Starts on:** Fourth beat. Count, "1, 2, 3," and then play.
> **Right Hand:** D above middle C
> **Left Hand:** D below middle C

SKYFALL

(from the Motion Picture *Skyfall*)

Words and Music by Adele Adkins and Paul Epworth

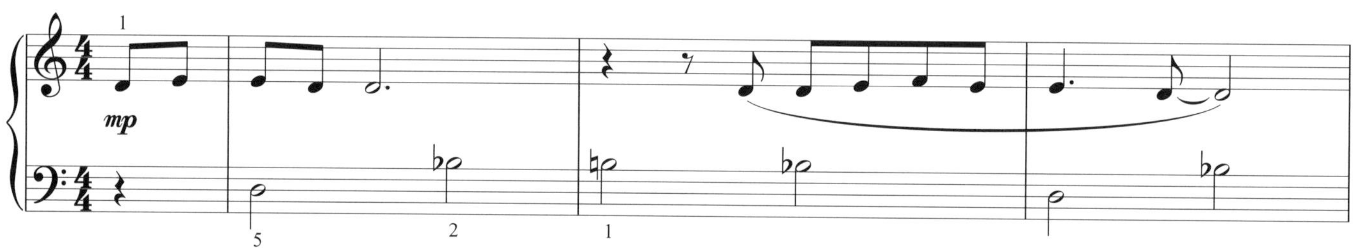

f

Technique Clinic 4

Exploring the Black Keys

1. Chromatics

When you move up or down by half step this is known as a **chromatic** sequence. (More on this later in the book.) You will need to contract the hand so that it's even smaller than the usual five-finger position. Take care with the change of time signature halfway through this exercise.

Track 76

2. Hot and Cold

In this exercise, you have almost the same sequence of notes in each group of two measures, but it sounds bright and happy the first time and sad the second. The proper way of describing the difference is that one is **major** and the other is **minor** (more about this in the next chapter).

Remember that sharps and flats are valid for a whole measure unless they are cancelled by a natural sign.

Track 77

3. Dotted Rhythms

Now play through the previous exercise again but with a dotted rhythm instead of a "straight" rhythm. Really strive for an even touch here.

Now we'll tie all these ideas together in a short piece:

Major versus Minor

Play the following five-note sequence:

Now play it again, with one crucial note changed:

What do you notice? Simply by lowering the E by a half step, you have gone from major to minor. You might say major sounds bright and happy, whereas minor sounds dull or sad. Listen to several different songs now and see if you can work out whether they are major or minor.

Have a look at the following groups of five notes.

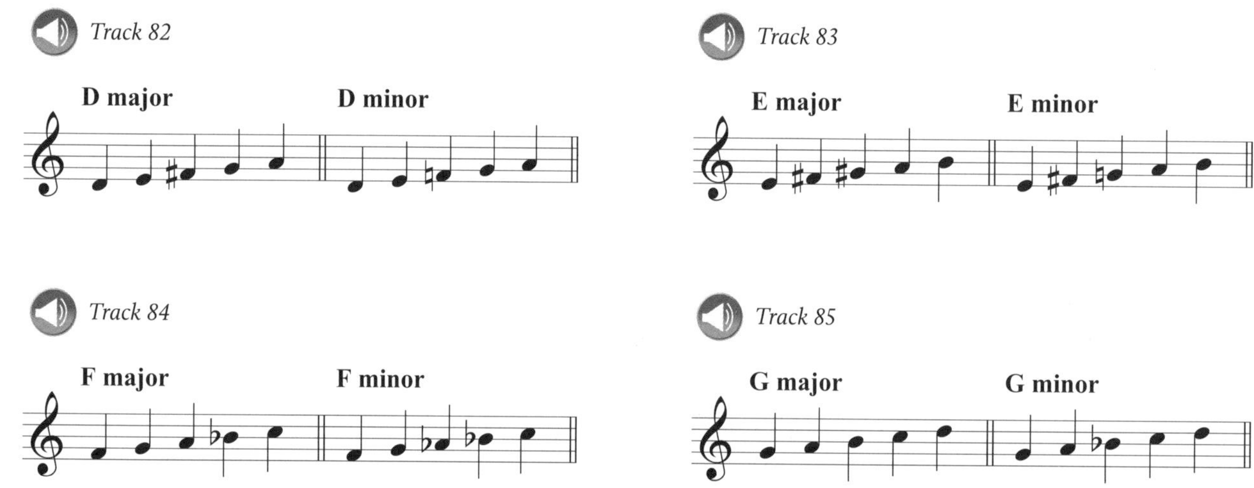

Notice that in some keys you need to use black notes in different places in the sequence to make them sound correct? Play through the following short extracts from songs and see if you can work out if they are major or minor.

CAN YOU FEEL THE LOVE TONIGHT?

(from *The Lion King*)

Music by Elton John

Lyrics by Tim Rice

EVERY BREATH YOU TAKE

Music and Lyrics by Sting

OLD TOWN ROAD (I GOT THE HORSES IN THE BACK)

Words and Music by Trent Reznor, Atticus Ross, Kiowa Roukema and Montero Lamar Hill

- Incorporates the song "34 Ghosts IV" (Words and Music by Atticus Ross and Trent Reznor)

Keys and Key Signatures

Although this represents a huge leap forward in your understanding of written music, in many ways it simplifies things: Rather than having a sharp or flat sign printed immediately in front of each note, a key signature has it permanently lodged in the margin:

All Fs are automatically F♯s—there is no need for the sharp sign to appear in front of every F.

Look at this song from the previous page. Here it is again, using a key signature.

CAN YOU FEEL THE LOVE TONIGHT?

(from *The Lion King*)
Music by Elton John
Lyrics by Tim Rice

The next one has the same key signature: All Fs are F♯s.

WRITING'S ON THE WALL

(from *Spectre*)
Words and Music by Sam Smith and James Napier

Here's a different key signature: B♭ in the margin. Now all Bs are automatically B♭s.

EIGHT DAYS A WEEK

Words and Music by John Lennon and Paul McCartney

The next song shares the same key signature: all Bs are B♭s.

EVERY BREATH YOU TAKE

Music and Lyrics by Sting

Compare this arrangement to the one you played on page 46. What do you notice? What has happened is the song has been put into a different key. On page 46, it is in D major but here it is in F major.

Keys

When we say that a song or piece of music is "in" a key, it means that there is a tonal center. The key note will be the most dominant note, the "home" note, if you like. A piece in G major centers around the note G.

On the next page, let's take a short extract from a song and see how it works in several different keys.

C major: no sharps or flats in the key signature. C is the "home" note.

WITH A LITTLE HELP FROM MY FRIENDS

Words and Music by John Lennon and Paul McCartney

Track 87

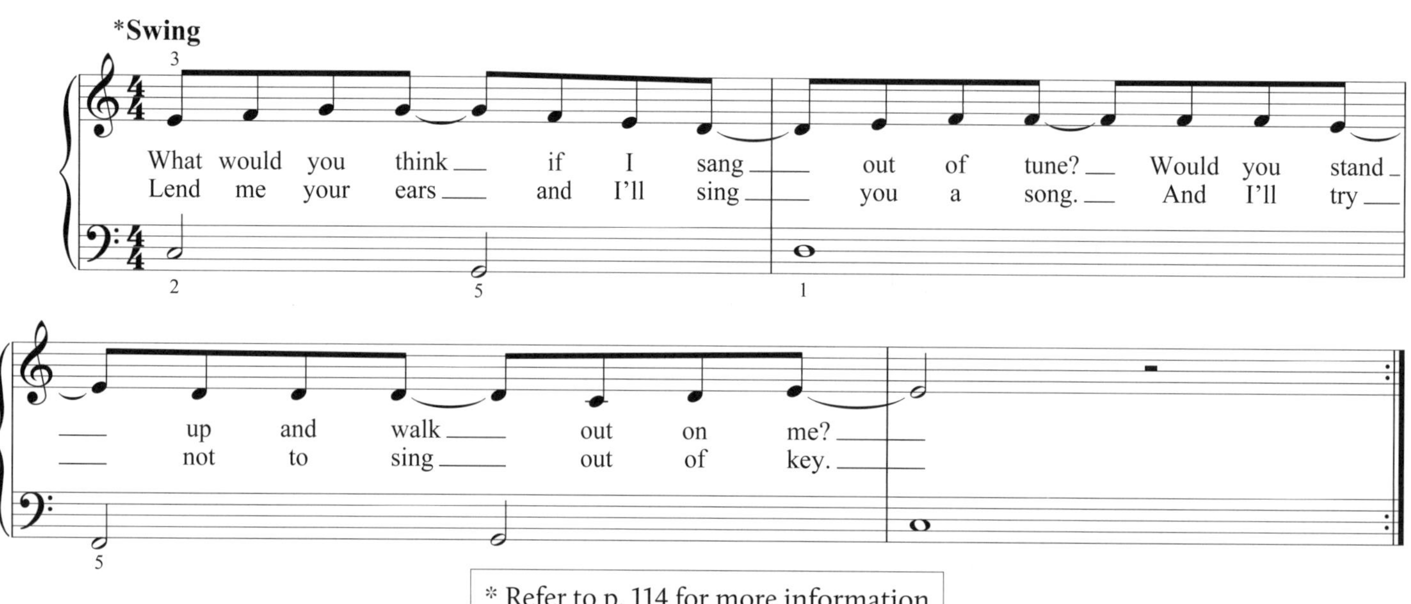

* Refer to p. 114 for more information

G major: F♯ in the key signature. G is the home note.

Track 88

F major: B♭ in the key signature. F is the home note.

Track 89

D major: F♯ and C♯ in the key signature. D is the home note.

Track 90

Moving music up and down through different keys is called **transposing**. Composers and arrangers transpose music into different keys according to the purpose of the music. It may be that a song in G major has a melody line that is just a little too high to sing. Transposing it down into D major could work better.

 **Do-It-Yourself**

The rhythm of this song is slightly different from what is printed: instead of "straight" eighth notes, the song has "swung" eighth notes, where in each pair of notes the first is lengthened and the second is shortened.

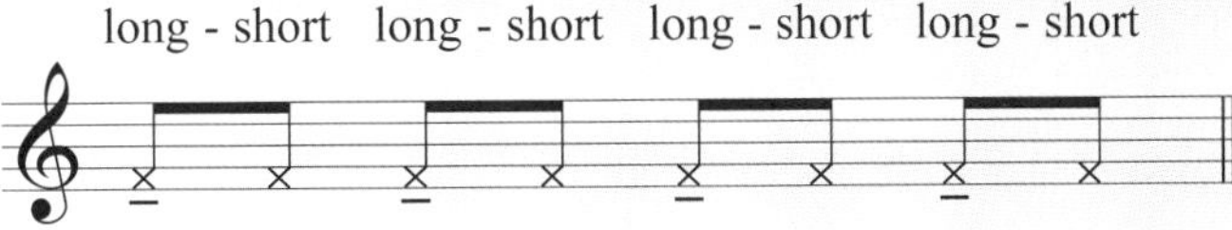

Have a listen to the song now to understand this rhythm. Here it is printed with the long eighth notes underlined and the short ones made smaller:

Track 91

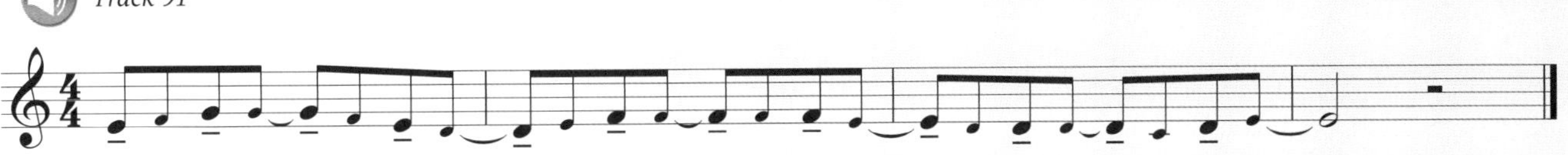

There is a whole chapter devoted to swing rhythm on page 115.

Now we'll take a closer look at the song that you played on page 78. Here's a longer version. It is in the key of E minor and the key signature states that all Fs are F♯s. The left hand is relatively simple throughout, although it does move up into the treble clef at measure 17. Take a moment to understand that the E in measure 17 is just above middle C. After four measures, in the treble clef, the left hand moves back down into the more familiar bass clef.

The Basics

Time Signature: 4/4 (four quarter notes per measure)
Starts on: First beat. Count, "1, 2, 3, 4," and then play.
Key: E minor (F♯ in the key signature)
Right Hand: F♯ over an octave above middle C
Left Hand: E over an octave below middle C

"Writing's on the Wall" appears on the next page to allow for easier reading.

WRITING'S ON THE WALL

(from *Spectre*)

Words and Music by Sam Smith and James Napier

Track 92

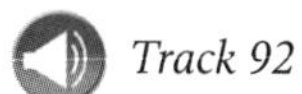

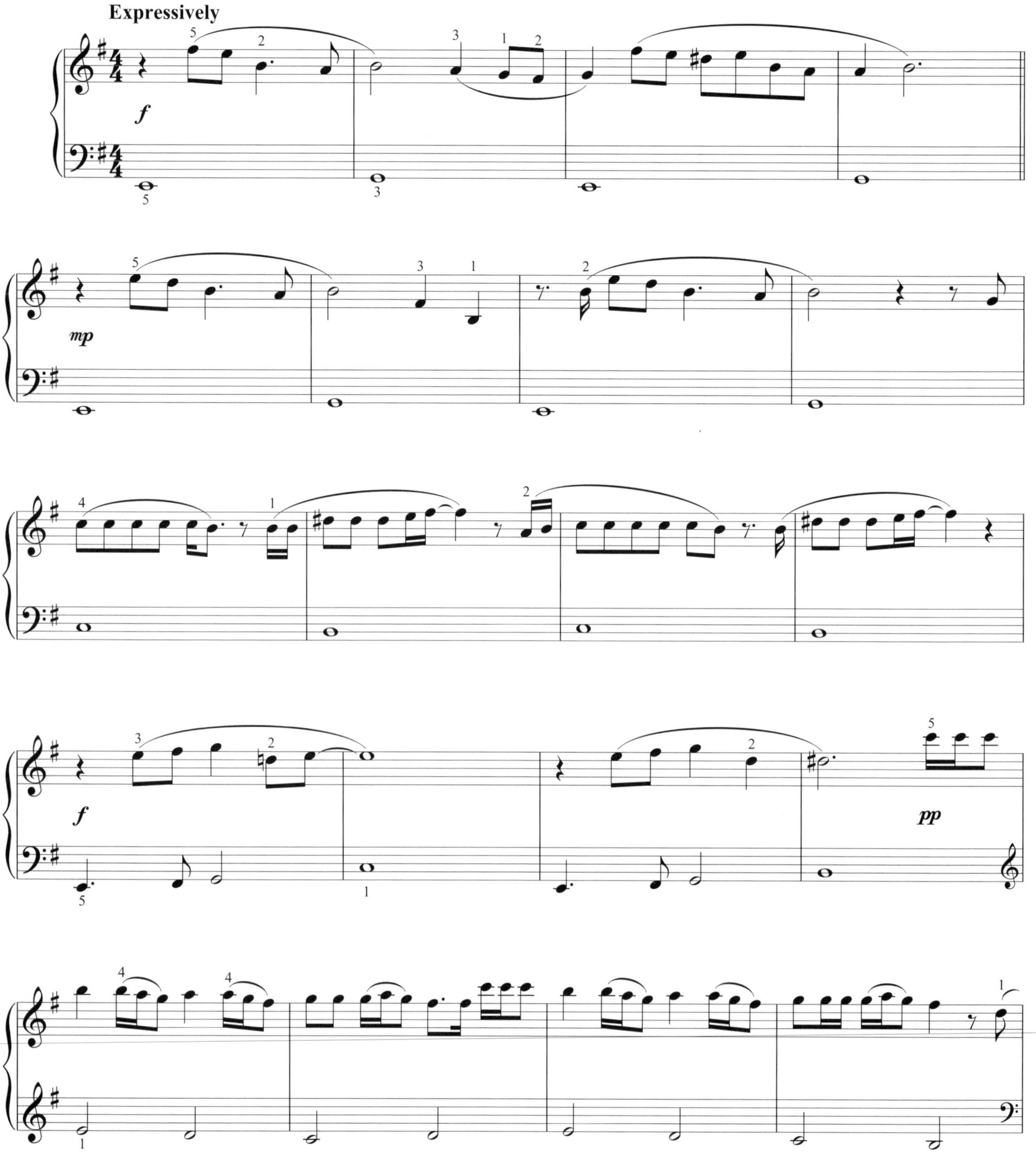
Expressively

* See below for more about this marking.

Tempo

At the beginning of a song, there will usually be an indication of the tempo (speed) of the music. Sometimes, it's simply an ordinary word, like "slow." Sometimes, particularly if it's a classical piece, you will find an Italian word. Here is a short table of the most common Italian tempo markings.

Largo or *Lento* or *Adagio*	slow
Andante or *Moderato*	at a steady "walking" pace
Allegretto	moderately fast
Allegro, Vivace, Presto	fast
Poco	a little
Rallentando or *rall.*	slow down
Ritardando or *rit.*	slow down
a. tempo	back to the original speed

Sometimes you get a **metronome mark**. A metronome mark gives the number of **beats per minute** (**bpm**). There is always a note value (often a quarter note) and a number.

♩ **= 60**	Steady; one beat per second
♩ **= 100**	Faster; driving forward
♩ **= 160**	Really fast

The Basics

Time Signature: 4/4 (four quarter notes per measure)
Starts on: Second beat. Count, "3, 4, 1," and then play.
Key: F major (B♭ in the key signature)
Right Hand: F above middle C
Left Hand: F below middle C

"Do You Want to Build a Snowman?" appears on the next page to allow for easier reading.

DO YOU WANT TO BUILD A SNOWMAN?

(from *Frozen*)

Music and Lyrics by Kristen Anderson-Lopez and Robert Lopez

Track 93

The next piece is in G—watch out for F♯s. It comes from Mozart's famous work *Eine Kleine Nachtmusik*. Try it hands separately first; the right hand has a lot to negotiate here, such as several hand positions, different note values and dotted rhythms. When you do put your hands together, you will need to work on the onset of the first three notes; the right-hand B and the left-hand G must sound exactly together, with a quarter rest in between.

The Basics

Time Signature: 4/4 (four quarter notes per measure)

Starts on: First beat. Count, "1, 2, 3, 4," and then play.

Key: G major (F♯ in the key signature)

Right Hand: B above middle C

Left Hand: G below middle C

EINE KLEINE NACHTMUSIK ("ROMANCE"), SECOND MOVEMENT

By Wolfgang Amadeus Mozart

Track 94

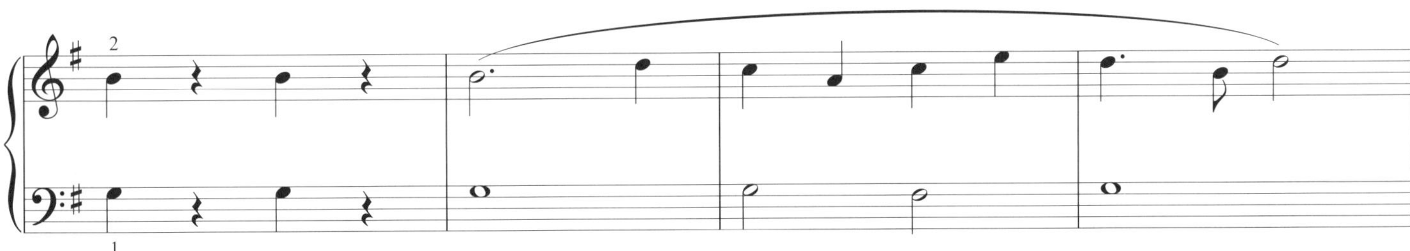

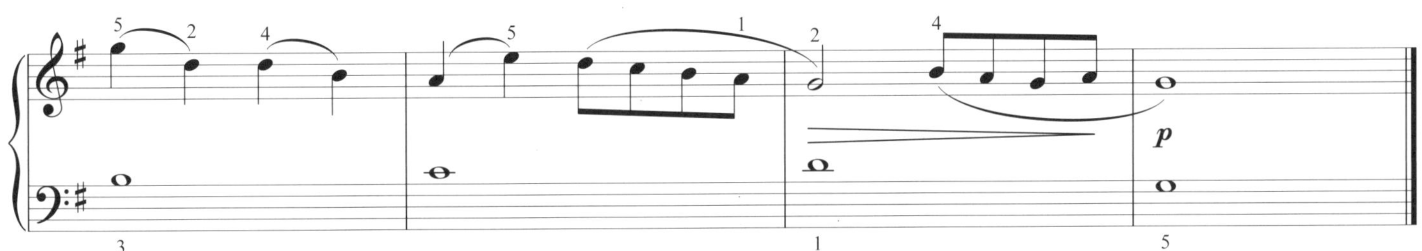

Chords

Filling Out the Harmony

So far, you've been playing pieces hands together, with one note in each hand. But this is only really an *outline* of harmony. It's possible to play several notes at once. Three notes together form a **chord**.

The Triad

A **triad** (group of three notes) is the simplest chord. It functions as a sort of building block.

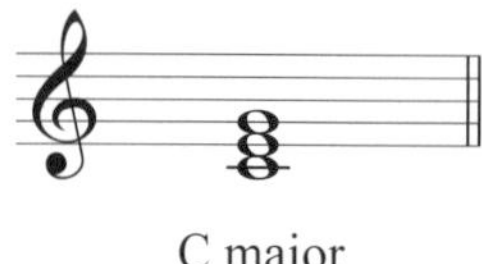

C major

This is a C major triad. But we can have chords of this shape anywhere on the keyboard.

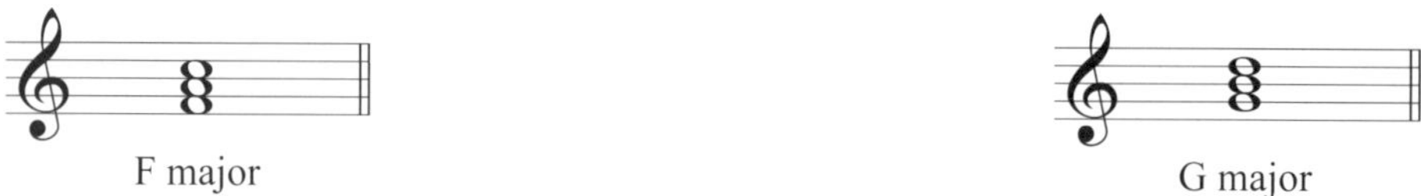

F major G major

Now, if we play triads up the keyboard from middle C with just the white notes, we get the following:

Track 95

D minor E minor F major G major A minor

Have you noticed that some of these chords are major and some are minor?

Some white-note triads will be minor, and to convert them into major triads, we need to need to raise the middle note by a half step.

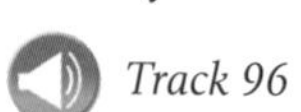

Track 96

D major E major A major

It's especially useful to get used to playing chords in the left hand, as you can then play a melody line in the right hand and accompany yourself with chords in the left hand.

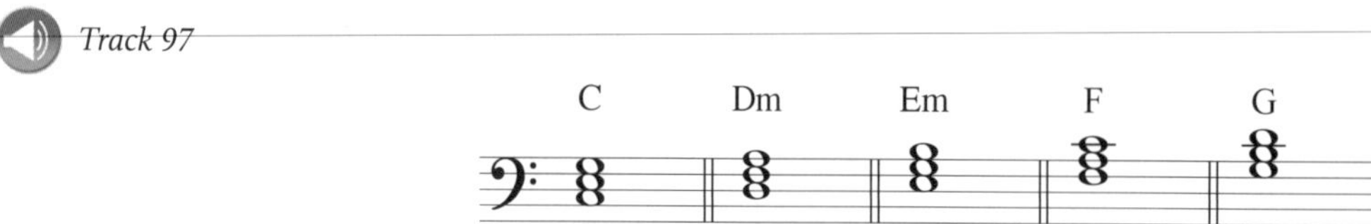

Play triads up and down the keyboard, with both hands, taking care to ensure all three notes sound exactly at the same time. This will take some practice.

Now let's take this idea and add some chords to songs you've recently played in the book. Instead of straight, single notes, the left hand is playing full triads. Practice the left hand first to get used to the shape of the chords and the shifts needed in between.

The chord names are written in between the two staffs with just a capital letter for a major chord and a small "m" to indicate a minor chord. It's good practice for you to get to know what the harmony is doing.

WRITING'S ON THE WALL

(from *Spectre*)

Words and Music by Sam Smith and James Napier

Track 98

The next song has half notes in the left hand. This means you're re-articulating the chord much more frequently and must really listen to get it together with the right-hand melody.

SHAKE IT OFF

Words and Music by Taylor Swift, Max Martin and Shellback

Track 99

Fingering

The simplest fingering to use for a triad is 1–3–5 in the left hand. But you may sometimes prefer to use 1–2–4. It depends on where the chord is and where you're moving to next—it's up to you. You're never obliged to use the fingering marked in the book, or indeed any music that you look at. The thing to do is to find the fingering that works for you and stick to it. Write it in on the music; you'll find you learn music much faster if you always use the same fingering.

WITH A LITTLE HELP FROM MY FRIENDS

Words and Music by John Lennon and Paul McCartney

➔ Do-It-Yourself

Why not try to put chords with some of the other songs you've played so far in this book? For example, this could be done with any of the following: "Edelweiss" (page 44), "Wonderwall" (page 48), "Beauty and the Beast" (page 53), the theme from *William Tell Overture* (page 57), "Colors of the Wind" (page 58), and the theme from *New World Symphony* (page 69). You could also try "With a Little Help from My Friends" in the other keys on page 80.

If there's a chord that doesn't quite sound right, either try a different one (you'll really need to use your ear) or just stick with the single note as before.

Mix It Up

Sometimes, a full triad is too much—the harmony sounds too thick. It may be that just two notes will do, particularly when the melody line is low and getting in the way of the accompaniment. Have a look at the following two songs:

LEAN ON ME

Words and Music by Bill Withers

Track 101

In "Away in a Manger," a chord of E minor would not have sounded quite right in measure 3, but removing the B and just playing two notes works okay. In measures 5–6, it's a little smoother and easier for the left hand to play triads followed by just two notes on the third beat.

AWAY IN A MANGER (THE CRADLE SONG)

Traditional Carol
Words by John T. McFarland (v.3)
Music by William J. Kirkpatrick

Left-Hand Drill

Before playing the next piece it's worth getting the hang of the left-hand chords first. Go back and forth between the following two chords, taking note of the fingerings.

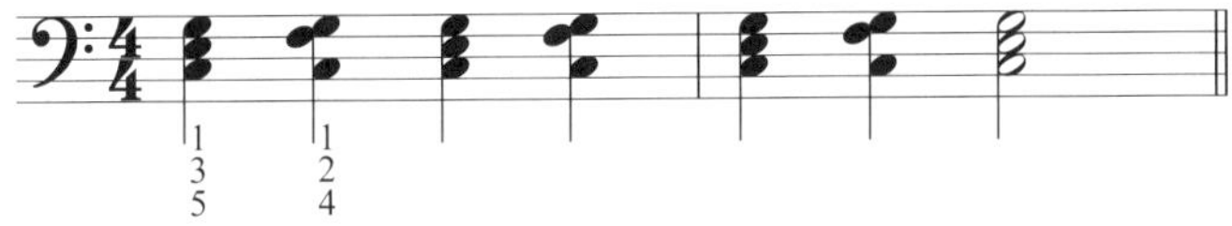

The Basics
Time Signature: 3/4 (three quarter notes per measure)
Starts on: Third beat. Count, "1, 2," and then play.
Key: C major
Right Hand: G above middle C
Left Hand: C major triad below middle C

"Quadrille" appears on the next page to allow for easier reading.

QUADRILLE

By Franz Joseph Haydn

Track 104

Right-Hand Drill

The next song has chords in the right hand and the tune in the left hand. Play the following chords with your right hand to get used to the different shapes. Take note of the B♭ in chords 2 and 3 and the C♯ in chord 4. The marked fingering is optional, but it should enable you to move smoothly from one shape to the next.

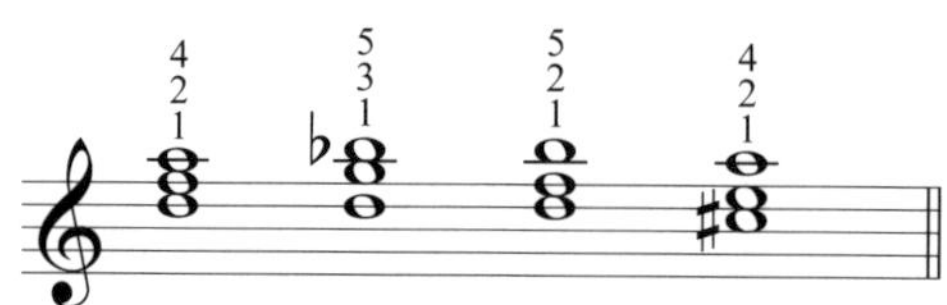

The Basics
Time Signature: 4/4 (four quarter notes per measure)
Starts on: First beat. Count, "1, 2, 3, 4," and then play.
Key: D minor (B♭ in the key signature)
Right Hand: D minor triad over an octave above middle C
Left Hand: D below middle C

BACK TO BLACK

Words and Music by Amy Winehouse and Mark Ronson

Technique Clinic 5

Playing Around with Chords

1. Alternating Between Two Chords

Make sure all three notes go down together and listen for an even touch; you don't want one note to dominate the chord. This is printed in the treble clef, but practice exactly the same exercise with the left hand, an octave lower. The fingering is marked for each hand, and you can repeat the switching as many times as you'd like before ending on the final chord.

Track 105

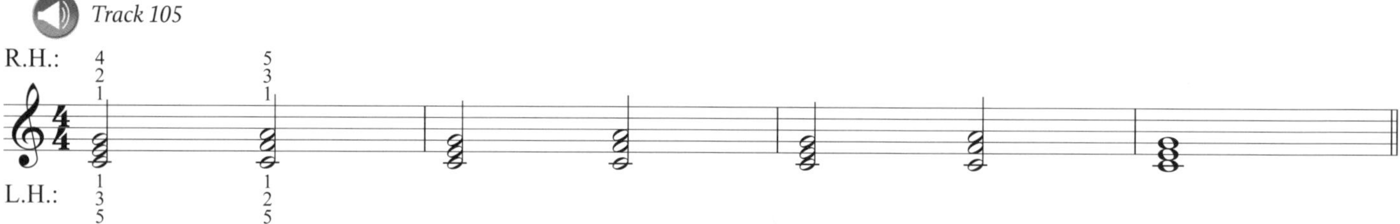

2. Bend and Stretch

This one is a little trickier, as the chords are constantly changing.

Track 106

3. Playing in 3rds

Try to play this as smoothly as possible, joining the notes together. Play through the motion as many times as you please.

Track 107

Track 108

Now we'll tie all these ideas together in a short piece. It's definitely worthwhile being able to play chords in several different keys and different positions, so this little tune is transposed into several keys. Some keys will be easier to play in than others. You have two options for fingering in the left hand, and it may depend on which key you are playing in. It's entirely up to you. Otherwise, try and keep the fingering the same through each one. Another big challenge here is the fact that one hand is playing legato (smoothly) while the other hand plays staccato (short and detached) chords. You could ignore this articulation until you're completely comfortable with the notes and playing hands together.

RISING FORTUNES

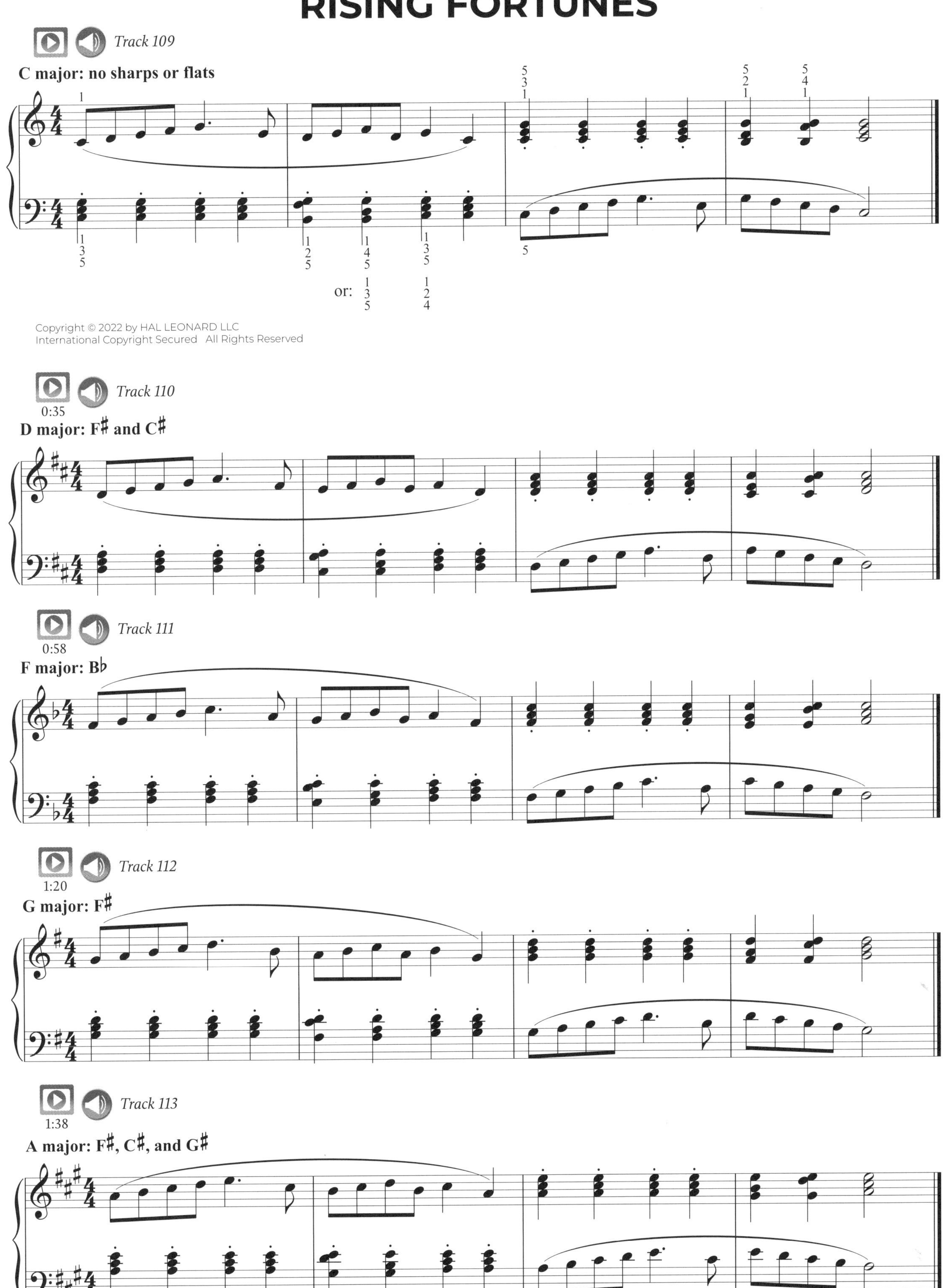

New Time Signatures

Counting in Eighth Notes

Remember how you learnt about time signatures way back at the beginning of the book i.e., 2/4, 3/4, and 4/4? The top number tells you how many beats to count in each measure, and the bottom number tells you what kind of note you are counting. The bottom number "4" means the music is based in quarter notes. If we change the bottom note to "8," then we are counting eighth notes. This means that a quarter note is now worth two beats! This involves quite a mind shift. Have a look at the following lines of music. In each case the time signature is based in eighth notes, and you can see the different ways of filling a measure.

You will see 3/8 frequently in classical music; 4/8 is not very common. 6/8 is very common in all types of music. When playing in 6/8, there are six eighth notes per measure. The notes are commonly grouped in threes, so you will have two groups of three in each measure. The strong beats are therefore beat 1 and beat 4 in each measure.

Try playing the following song extract.

NEVER TEAR US APART

Words and Music by Andrew Farriss and Michael Hutchence

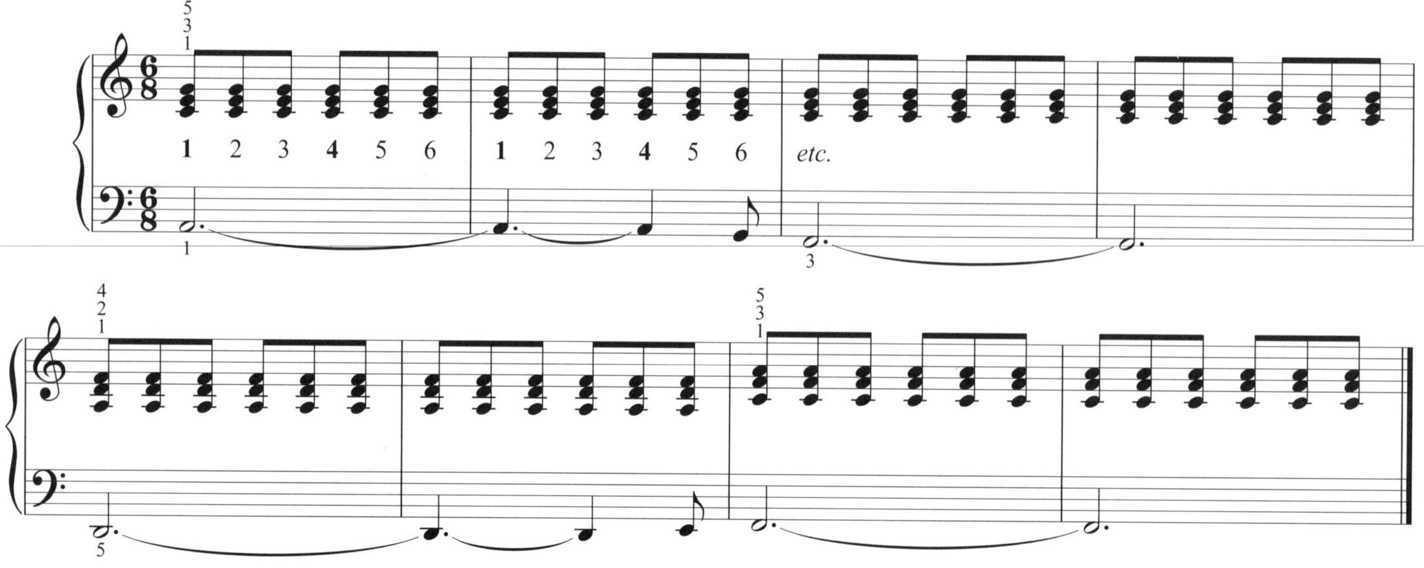

Sometimes, you have notes tied over the middle of the measure, which makes it a little harder to count. Here, you really have to *feel* the meter underneath the notes.

WE ARE THE CHAMPIONS

Words and Music by Freddie Mercury

Drill

For the next song, "Feeling Good," you should play through the first line, reprinted here, as a warm-up. This will get you used to counting in units of six, but with the strong beats on 1 and 4, as above. The left hand plays dotted quarter notes to emphasize this.

The **accent** indicates that the note should be played with extra force.

or

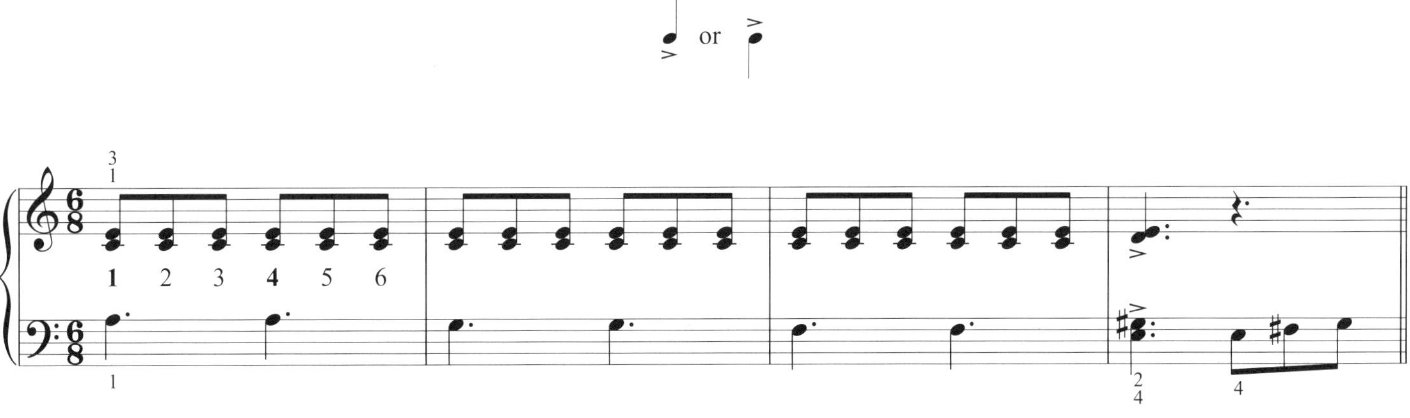

The Basics
Time Signature: 6/8 (six eighth notes per measure)
Starts on: First beat. Count, "1, 2, 3, 4, 5, 6," and then play.
Key: A minor (no key signature)
Right Hand: Middle C and E
Left Hand: A below middle C

"Feeling Good" appears on the next page to allow for easier reading.

FEELING GOOD

(from *The Roar of the Greasepaint - The Smell of the Crowd*)

Words and Music by Leslie Bricusse and Anthony Newley

The Broken Chord

A **broken chord** is simply a chord that has been broken down into single notes, in a recurring pattern:

Track 117

This is an extract from the famous *Moonlight Sonata* by Beethoven. The right hand plays broken chords throughout. Read the notes carefully; there is a B♭ in the key signature and several other sharps and flats. Also, I used the sustain pedal in Track 118B (more on this later).

PIANO SONATA NO. 14, OP. 27, NO. 2 ("MOONLIGHT")

Left-Hand Drills

In the next song, the left hand plays broken chords throughout. It's useful to play the following as solid chords first to get used to the shape and then to break them down into broken chords.

G7/F

TOOLBOX

When playing in 6/8, you often have this rhythm:

This is a lilting rhythm that has a real sense of forward movement. It's very common in nursery rhymes, e.g., "Here We Go 'Round the Mulberry Bush," "Girls and Boys Come Out to Play," "Humpty Dumpty," etc. You will see many examples of this rhythm in the right hand of the following song. Take a moment to understand the complicated song structure: There are two sets of repeats, each with first- and second-time measures. In Track 123B, I used the sustain pedal for a smoother, flowing sound.

The Basics
Time Signature: 6/8 (six eighth notes per measure)
Starts on: First beat. Count, "1, 2, 3, 4, 5, 6," and then play.
Key: C major (no key signature)
Right Hand: E above middle C

O HOLY NIGHT

French Words by Placide Cappeau
English Words by John S. Dwight
Music by Adolphe Adam

Track 123A
Track 123B

1.
2.
mp
f
rit.
p

➔ Do-It-Yourself

Notice the names written above the chords in the left-hand drills above: F/C, G/B, etc.? You learned in the chapter about chords that a capital letter simply meant a major chord, so F would be:

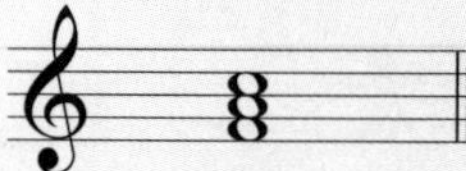

But if we rearranged the same three notes so that the top note is on the bottom, we get this:

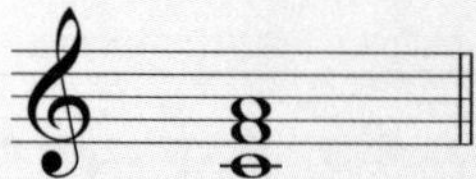

This new chord is known as F/C ("F over C") because C is the bottom note. Look at the following table:

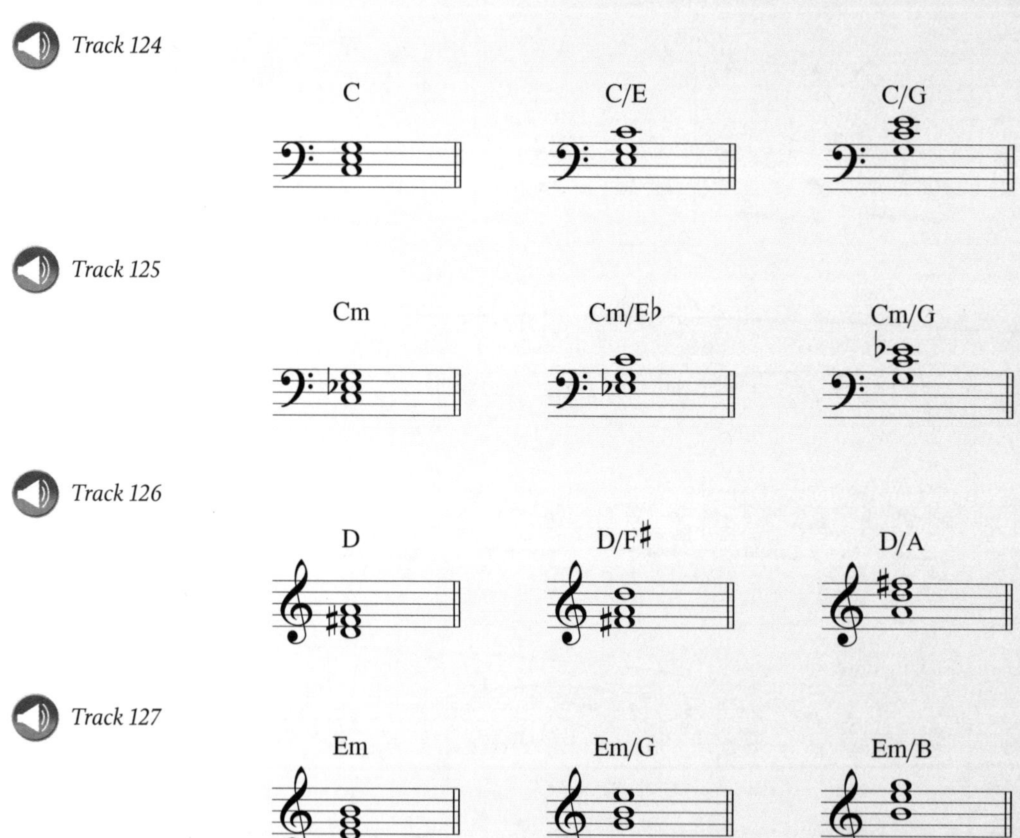

Try playing these chords—you can hear that the variations are still really the same chord, as they have the same three notes, but the altered position gives greater variety.

Understanding this concept will help you to read chord charts that you may see in music books.

(There is a longer list of chords in Appendix 2.)

Scales and Arpeggios

Important Musical Patterns

Many pop songs and lots of classical pieces have scale passages in them, so it's worth getting to know the scale pattern. We'll start with C major: no sharps or flats, next-door notes from C ascending to the next C (an octave). Here's the standard fingering pattern (the left hand has been transposed an octave down):

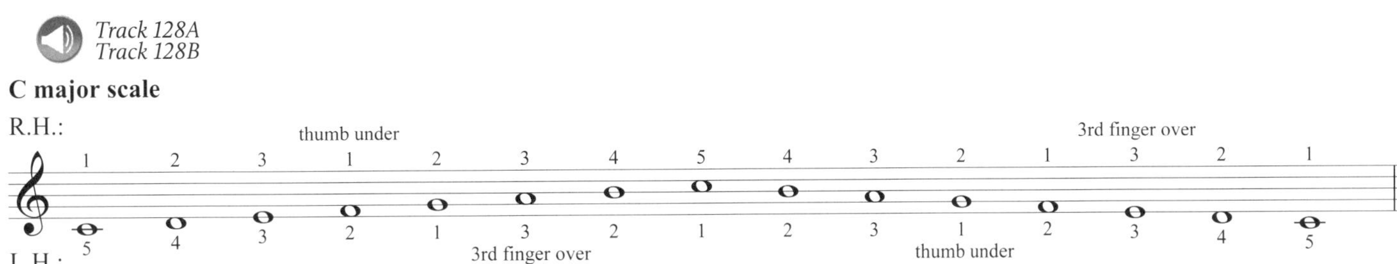

Right hand: Start with your thumb. Move your thumb underneath your second and third fingers, so that it reappears on the F. On the way down, you do the opposite: after playing the F you move your third finger over to the E. Try to execute these transitions as smoothly as you possibly can.

Left hand: Start with your fifth finger. Move your third finger over your thumb on the way up, and put your thumb under on the way down.

Here are two more major scales, each with sharps and flats all written in. The fingering pattern is the same for each scale.

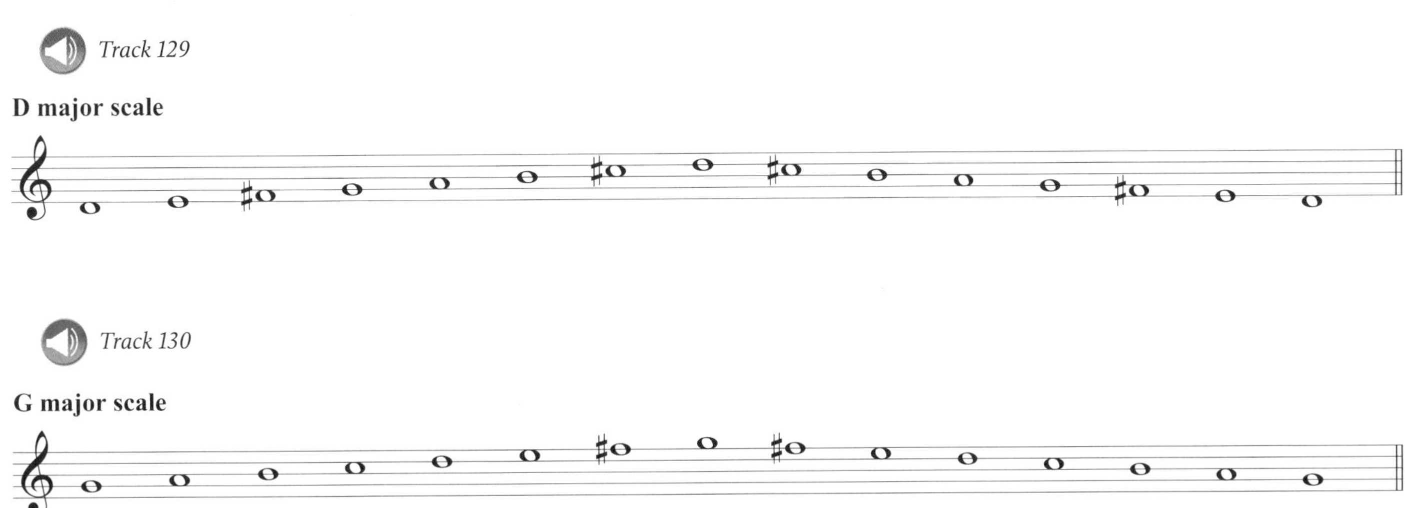

If you've played them correctly, they should "sound the same" in the sense that they are all following the same pattern of whole steps and half steps.

The Minor Scale

The **minor** scale has a different pattern of whole steps and half steps. For the following scales, the standard fingering pattern is exactly the same as for the major scale. Turn to the next page to see an example.

A minor scale

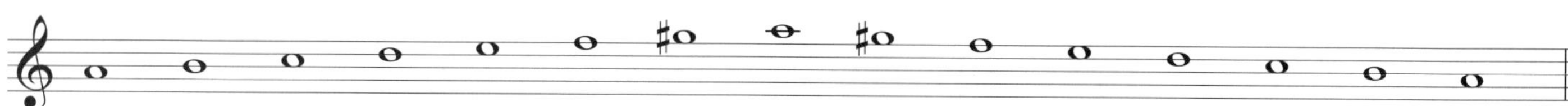

(There are more scales in the online supplements.)

The following song has a descending scale in the right hand.

CAN CAN

(from *Orpheus in the Underworld*)

By Jacques Offenbach

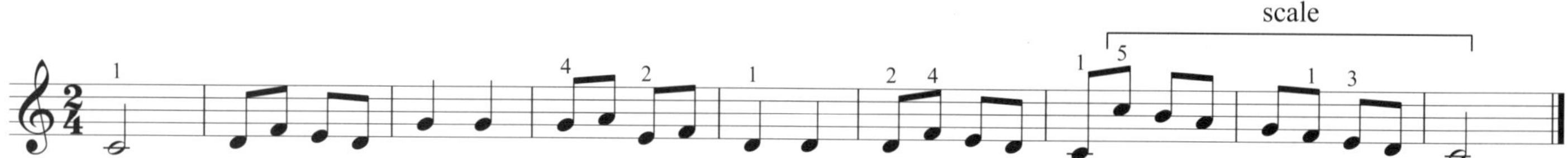

This bass line of this song is a slow descending scale.

PIANO MAN

Words and Music by Billy Joel

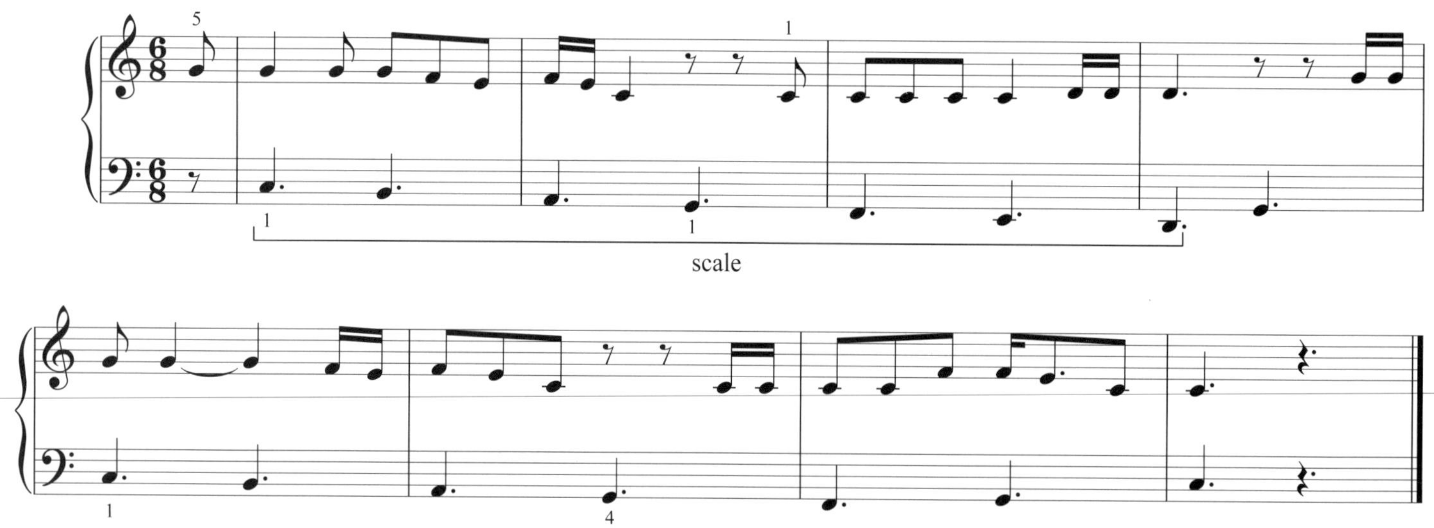

The next song extract is full of scales in the left hand.

THE MAN WHO SOLD THE WORLD

Words and Music by David Bowie

The next piece has several scales that go up as high as the fifth scale degree. This is in G major—watch out for F♯s.

Right-Hand Drill

As this is the main theme from the piece you need to get the hang of it with the right hand before attempting anything else. Try to play the eighth notes evenly, and keep your wrist relaxed.

Track 133

The Basics
Time Signature: 3/4 (three quarter notes per measure)
Starts on: First beat. Count, "1, 2, 3," and then play.
Key: G major (F# in the key signature)
Right Hand: D over an octave above middle C
Left Hand: G and B below middle C

MINUET IN G MAJOR, BWV ANH. 114

(from *Notebook for Anna Magdalena Bach*)

By Christian Petzold

Track 134

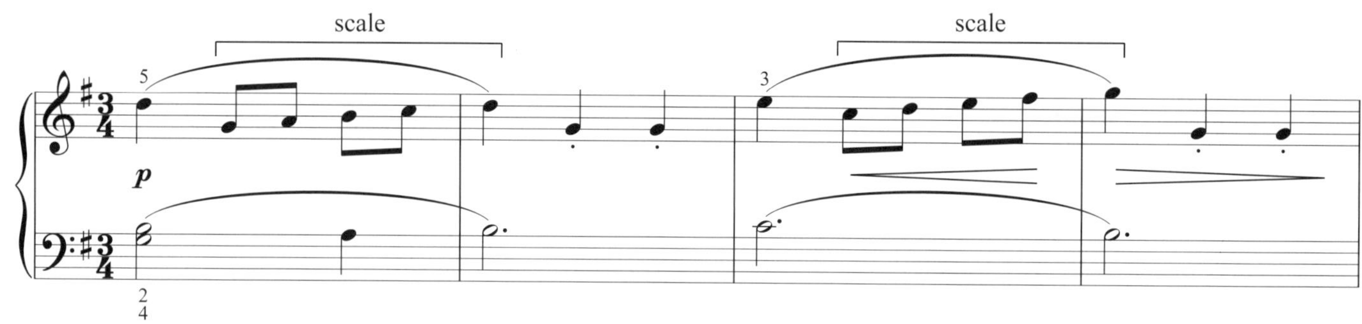

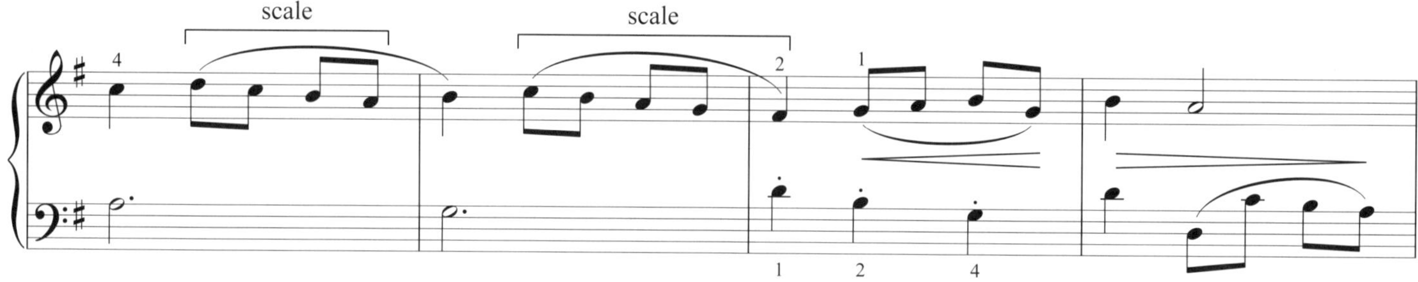

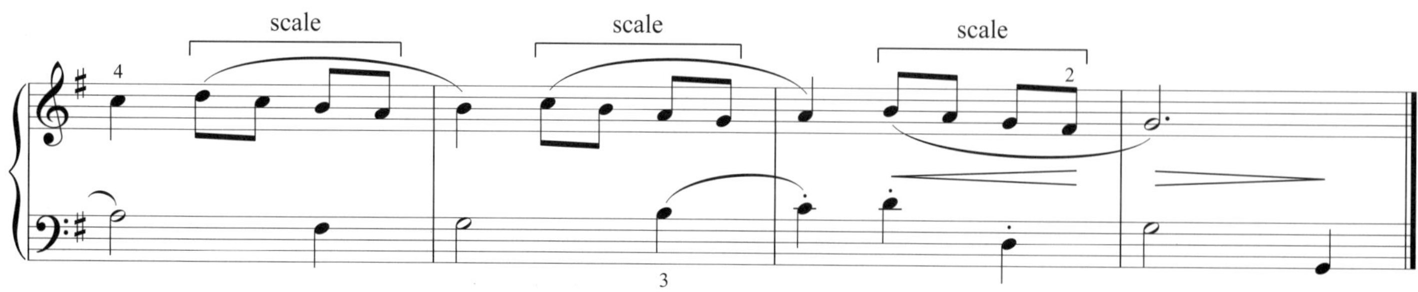

Now we return to "Yesterday" by the Beatles. This is a fuller version, and it features several partial scales in both hands.

TOOLBOX

This song introduces a new concept: **D.C. al Coda**. This means you should go back to the "head" (beginning) until the **coda**. When you get to the "to coda" sign (⊕), you skip the repeat and go straight to the ending.

The Basics

Time Signature: 4/4 (four quarter notes per measure)
Starts on: First beat. Count, "1, 2, 3, 4," and then play.
Key: F major (B♭ in the key signature)
Right Hand: G above middle C
Left Hand: F and A below middle C

YESTERDAY

Words and Music by John Lennon and Paul McCartney

Track 135

> **➔ Do-It-Yourself**
> Rather than use a full scale, many pieces and songs use just a part of a scale in the melody line, e.g., just five notes, which also happen to fit neatly within the five-finger position.
>
> Can you think of any pieces or songs that you've played elsewhere in the book that use part-scale passages? For example, "Lean On Me" has C–D–E–F; what about "Deck the Halls," "I've Got My Eye on You," etc.?
>
> Try to spot scale patterns in other songs that you listen to.

Arpeggios

Arpeggios are very similar to broken chords. We simply go one note further; up to the octave.

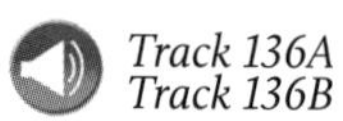

Track 136A
Track 136B

C major arpeggio

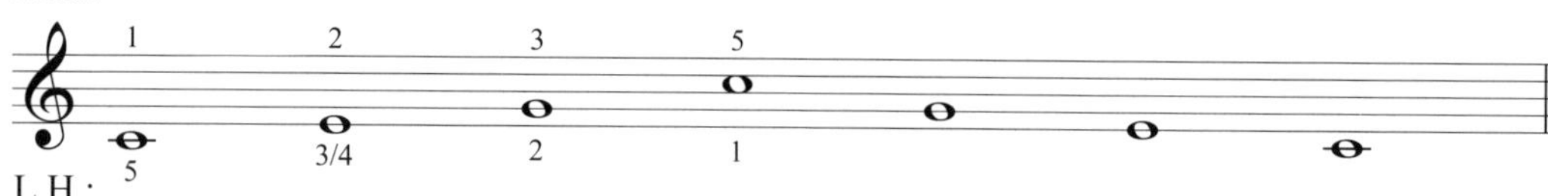

You need to spread the hand out a little further than usual. Don't feel you have to cover the whole octave, though. Move your elbow out to the right as you go up the arpeggio, then back again as you come down. This way, the arm movement will help the hand.

Here are some more examples:

Track 137

F major arpeggio

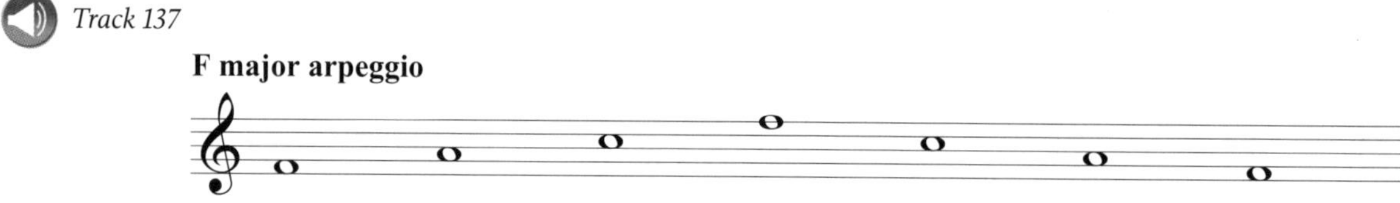

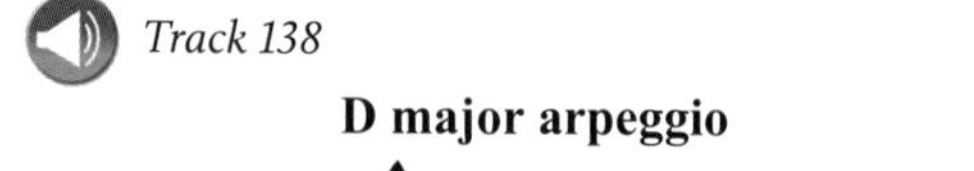

Track 138

D major arpeggio

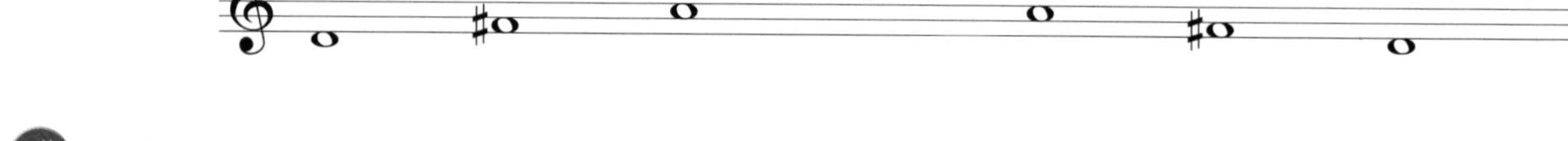

Track 139

G major arpeggio

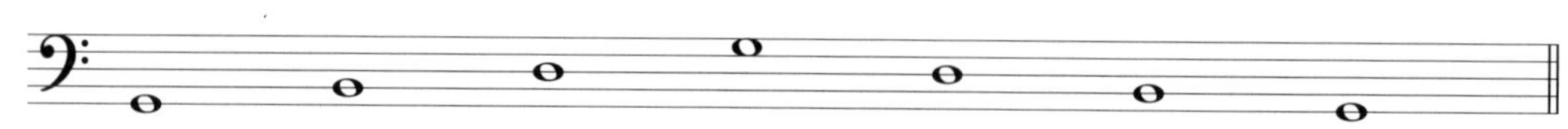

Track 140

A major arpeggio

> **Piano Talk**
> Steinway is considered to be one of the best piano brands. The Steinway family has been making pianos since 1853.

Here are some examples of songs containing arpeggio figures. You will see that the top note isn't always present. Often, the texture will consist of a partial arpeggio.

EVERYBODY HURTS

Words and Music by William Berry, Peter Buck, Michael Mills and Michael Stipe

In this song, the right hand has a repeating rhythmic riff, more akin to a broken chord pattern.

CLOCKS

Words and Music by Guy Berryman, Jon Buckland, Will Champion and Chris Martin

Both hands have arpeggio patterns here:

OB-LA-DI, OB-LA-DA

Words and Music by John Lennon and Paul McCartney

➔ Do-It-Yourself

For the next song you could practice your left-hand arpeggios in the following keys: F, Am, B♭, Gm, A, Dm, D♭. Just put your fifth finger on the key note and space out your hand so that it forms the same shape as the other arpeggios, and away you go!

Note that in the intro the right hand starts in the bass clef. There is a small treble clef in the middle of measure 4, so at this point, the right hand changes back to the treble clef. (I used the sustain pedal on Track 141B for a smoother, flowing sound.)

The Basics
Time Signature: 6/8 (six eighth notes per measure)
Starts on: First beat. Count, "1, 2, 3, 4, 5, 6," and then play.
Key: F major (B♭ in the key signature)
Right Hand: F below middle C
Left Hand: F over an octave below middle C

WHAT A WONDERFUL WORLD

Words and Music by George David Weiss and Bob Thiele

Track 141A
Track 141B

The next piece combines arpeggios and broken chord figures. It is the well-known *Für Elise* by Beethoven. We just look at an arrangement of the first section on page 64.

Drills

Firstly, you need to play arpeggios that start in the left hand and move through to the right hand.

 *Track 142*

Note that in the first one, the left-hand C is missed out—stretch your hand out over an octave. Aim to play this legato; there should be no bump when you change hands.

In the second one, the right hand imitates the left hand exactly.

 *Track 143*

Let's put these two ideas together. Here the hands need to work together as they overlap each other.

Track 144

There are some technical challenges: Work on strengthening your fourth and fifth fingers for this next exercise. Try and keep your hand steady and remember to support your wrist. (Again, I used the sustain pedal in Track 146B for a smoother sound.)

 *Track 145*

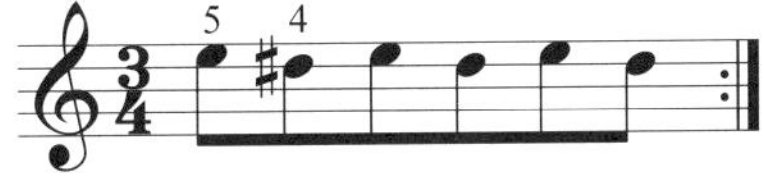

The Basics

Time Signature: 3/4 (three quarter notes per measure)
Starts on: Third beat. Count, "1, 2," and then play.
Key: A minor (no key signature)
Right Hand: E over an octave above middle C
Left Hand: A over an octave below middle C

"Für Elise" appears on the next page to allow for easier reading.

FÜR ELISE, WOO 59

By Ludwig van Beethoven

> **➔ Do-It-Yourself**
> Look at earlier songs in the book that have arpeggio patterns, e.g., "Do You Want to Build a Snowman?," the themes from *William Tell Overture*, *Surprise Symphony*, and *Eine Kleine Nachtmusik*. See if you can spot arpeggio patterns in other songs that you listen to.

Of course, the reality is that most music combines lots of these different patterns. Now that you're aware of them have a look at the following song. This is the intro to "Piano Man," which we looked at in the scales chapter. It has examples of chords, scales, and arpeggios.

PIANO MAN

Words and Music by Billy Joel

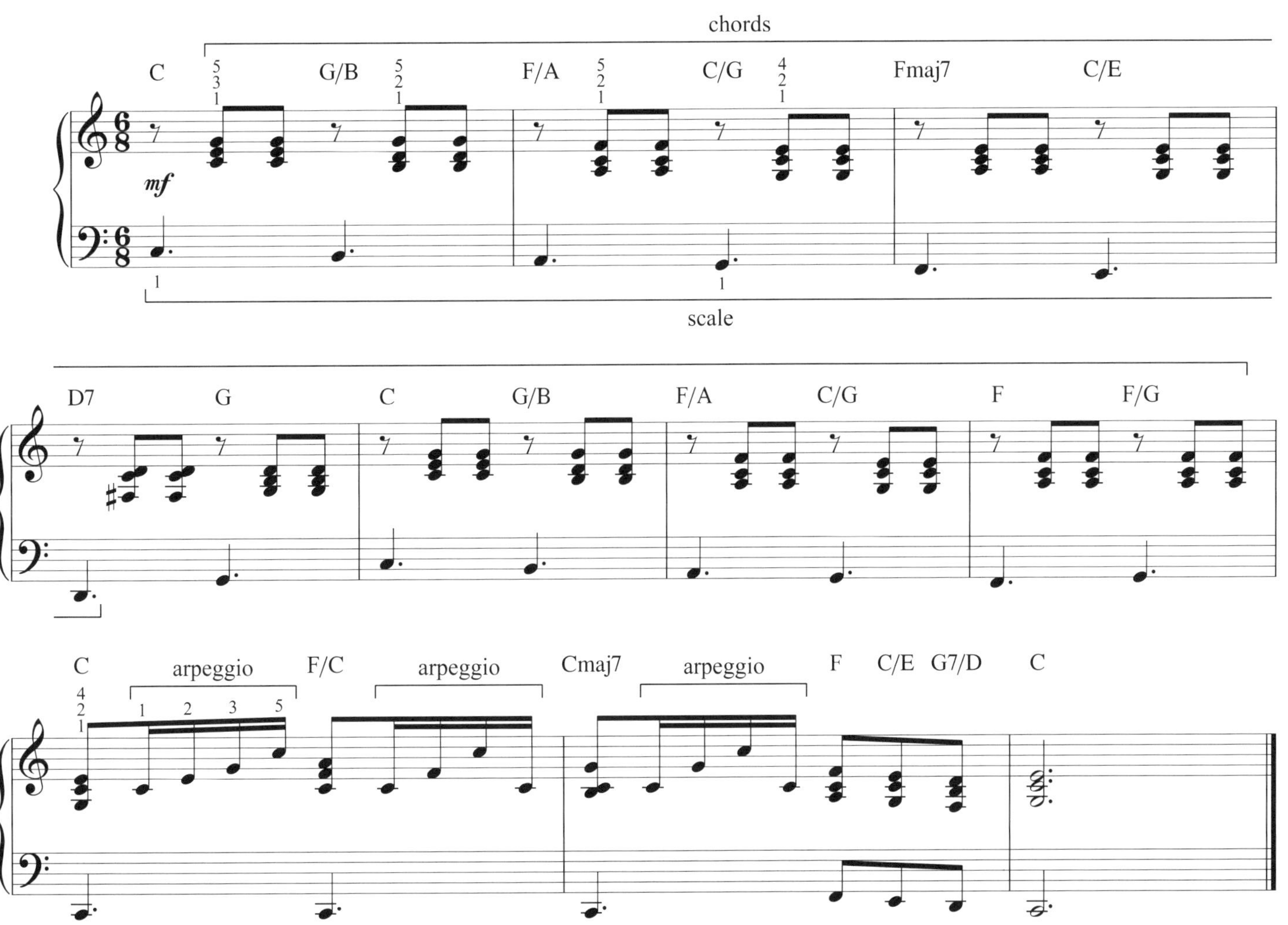

> **Piano Talk**
> Roland contributed to the development of the **MIDI** specification (Musical Instrument Digital Interface) and brought the first digital piano to market in 1983.

Technique Clinic 6

Scales and Arpeggios

1. Scales up to the 5th

Play through the same musical pattern, moving through the different keys from C to D, E, F, and G. Use the same fingering for each one. This is a useful exercise to warm up your fingers when you start a practice session.

Track 147

2. Arpeggios Revisted

Keep your wrists relaxed; your arms will quickly tire if you tense up.

Track 148

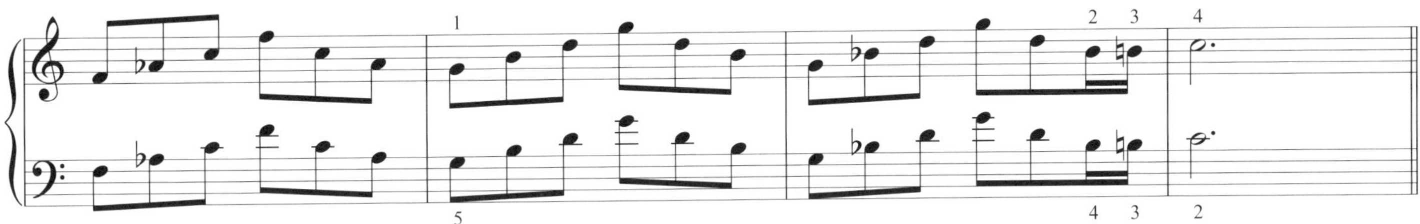

Now we'll tie these two figures together in the following piece.

RAGS TO RICHES

Track 149

Exploring New Rhythms

Swing

This idea is mentioned in a DIY box on page 81, when we looked at "With a Little Help from My Friends." "Back to Black" also uses swing rhythms. It is an important concept that deserves further exploration. You will find swing rhythm in lots of pop and jazz songs. Essentially, it is a distortion of the printed rhythm so that the first in each pair of eighth notes is lengthened and the second is shortened.

Drill

You will see a measure that looks like this:

You need to think like this:

and it sounds like this:

Tap the asterisked beats with your left hand while tapping the notes with your right hand. Once you're comfortable doing this, drop your left hand out and keep your right hand going. This is what swing rhythm feels like. The difficulty is being able to understand and reproduce this rhythm while looking at a different one.

The following tunes all have swung eighth notes.

MOONDANCE

Words and Music by Van Morrison

RAINDROPS KEEP FALLIN' ON MY HEAD

(from *Butch Cassidy and the Sundance Kid*)

Lyrics by Hal David

Music by Burt Bacharach

ISN'T SHE LOVELY

Words and Music by Stevie Wonder

Spend a lot of time getting to know the right hand before attempting to put the next one together. The rhythm is quite tricky, and remember that the eighth notes are swung.

The Basics

Time Signature: 4/4 (four quarter notes per measure)
Starts on: First beat. Count, "1, 2, 3, 4," and then play.
Key: F major (B♭ in the key signature)
Right Hand: A above middle C
Left Hand: F over an octave below middle C

"You've Got a Friend in Me" appears on the next page to allow for easier reading.

YOU'VE GOT A FRIEND IN ME

(from *Toy Story*)

Music and Lyrics by Randy Newman

The final piece in this chapter is an arrangement of a well-known jazz piece by Miles Davis. It uses swung eighth notes, but is in 3/4. It is in G major, but the left hand plays F♮s throughout, so the key signature is more of an identity.

Drills

The left hand spends most of the piece playing this riff. You need to extend your thumb out to the F♮ each time. If you have a big hand, you can try the alternative fingering.

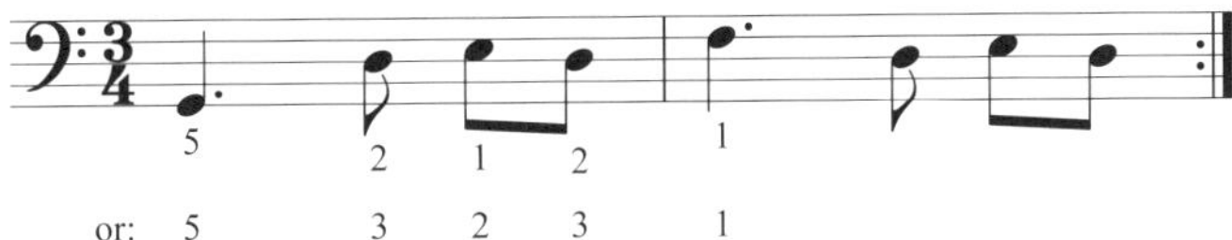

Now find the notes of these two chords. They involve an interesting clash between, firstly, the F♮ and the F♯, and then in the second one between the G♭ and the G♮. This is a jazzy dissonance that has a very distinctive color. It is also known as a **chromatic shift** (more on this in the next chapter).

Try to join the notes together as smoothly as you can as you go back and forward over the chords.

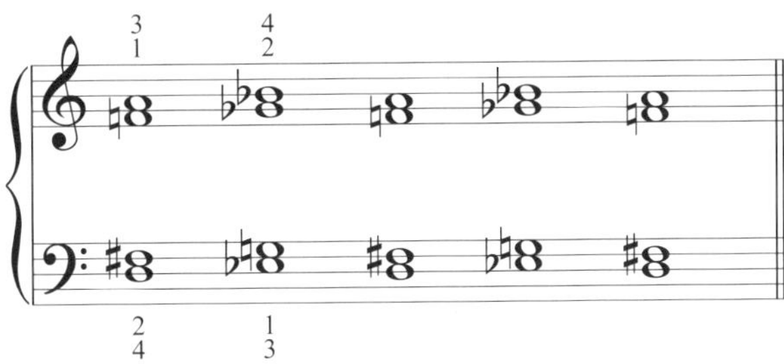

> **The Basics**
> **Time Signature:** 3/4 (three eighth notes per measure)
> **Starts on:** First beat. Count, "1, 2, 3," and then play.
> **Key:** G major (F♯ in the key signature)
> **Right Hand:** D above middle C
> **Left Hand:** G over an octave below middle C

"All Blues" appears on the next page to allow for easier reading.

ALL BLUES

By Miles Davis

More Work with the Black Keys

Chromaticism

Chromatic comes from the Greek word **chroma**, which means "color." Essentially, it is the insertion of half steps into ordinary major or minor passages, giving an unexpected and colorful twist to a melody line. The chromatic scale moves in half steps. It is neither major nor minor.

Track 152

We therefore talk of "chromatic" movement in music: moving up or down in half steps.

BILLS

Words and Music by Gamal Lewis, Rickard Göransson, Jacob Hindlin and Eric Frederic

Watch out for sharps in the next one, both in the key signature and during the piece itself. The first note in measure 2 is an E♯ (the same as F♮).

IN THE HALL OF THE MOUNTAIN KING

(from *Peer Gynt*)
By Edvard Grieg

Track 153

Right-Hand Drill

"Rolling in the Deep" by Adele has a very chromatic melody line. Play through the following exercise, taking care to get the fingering right. You need to contract your hand a little, so that fingers 3, 4, and 5 are close together. Then, when you play the song, you should always have your fourth finger on the G#.

Track 154

> **The Basics**
> **Time Signature:** 4/4 (four quarter notes per measure)
> **Starts on:** First beat. Count, "1, 2, 3, 4," and then play.
> **Key:** D minor (B♭ in the key signature)
> **Right Hand:** A above middle C
> **Left Hand:** D below middle C

ROLLING IN THE DEEP

Words and Music by Adele Adkins and Paul Epworth

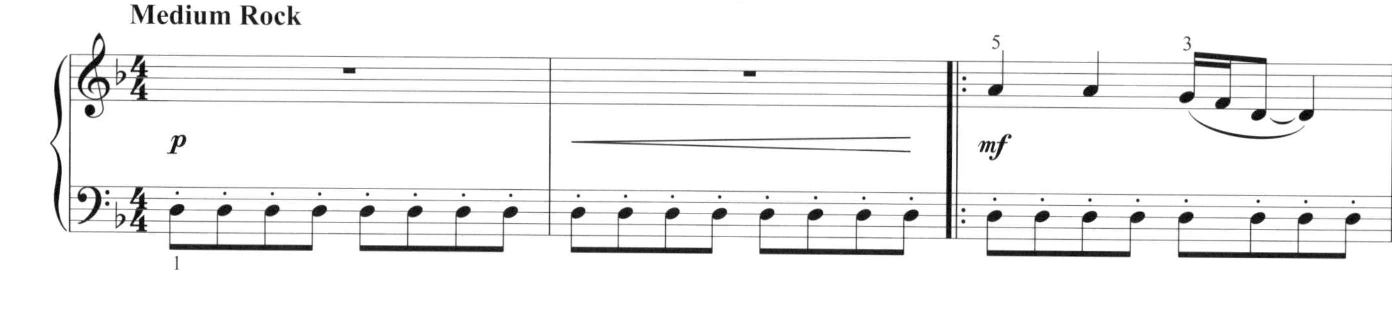

1.
2.

The next piece is a jazz classic: "Take Five" by Paul Desmond and made famous by the Dave Brubeck Quartet. The piece gets its title from the meter: five beats per measure. This gives it a quirky, distinctive feel, especially when combined with the swing rhythm and the very chromatic melody line.

Drills

The intro sets up what the left hand plays for most of the piece. Play through the left hand on its own first, to get the hang of the swing rhythm. Here the second pair of eighth notes is different rhythmically from the first, on account of the fact that the long eighth note on beat 2 is a rest. Then, add the right hand, which is simply playing the top notes of each chord. Make sure your hands are exactly together.

Track 155

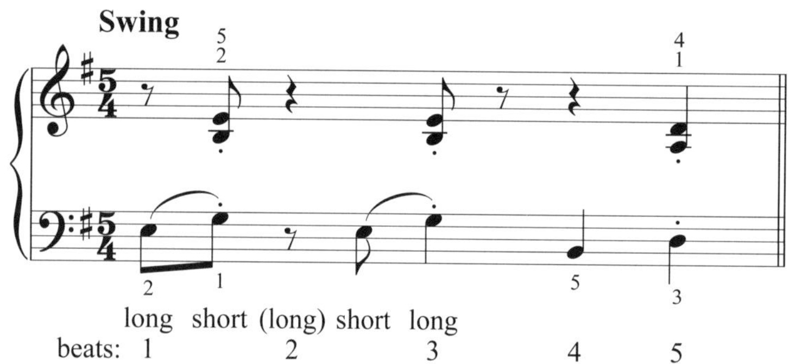

Next, you need to decide on your fingering for the main riff. This is the most recognizable bit of the piece, so it's worth spending some time getting it right. Either move your third finger over your fourth as neatly as you can, or bring your thumb under. Remember that it's swung, so your eighth notes need to go, "long-short, long-short," etc.

Track 156

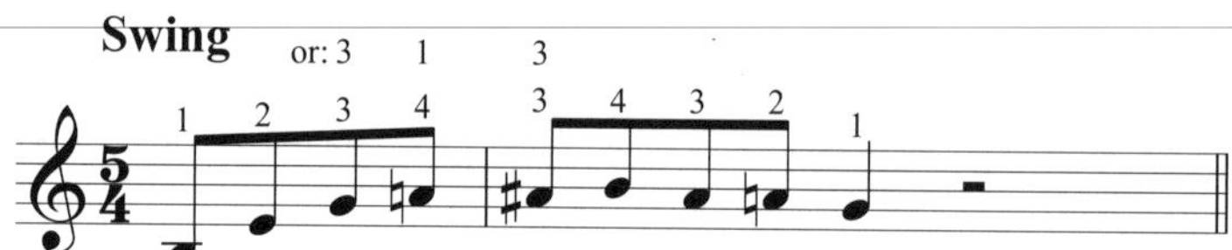

There are lots of staccato dots in the piece, often at the ends of slurs. Here the phrase of (even) 16th notes ends with a staccato quarter note. The staccato dot really turns the quarter note into a 16th with rests after. Make sure both hands arrive at the second beat together.

Track 157

Piano Talk
In 2015, Steinway created the "Fibonacci," a piano whose spiral patterns were inspired by the spirals generated from the mathematical Fibonacci sequence, nature's "golden ratio."

The Basics

Time Signature: 5/4 (five quarter notes per measure)
Starts on: First beat. Count, "1, 2, 3, 4, 5," and then play.
Key: E minor (F♯ in the key signature)
Right Hand: B and E around middle C
Left Hand: E below middle C

"Take Five" appears on the next page to allow for easier reading.

TAKE FIVE

By Paul Desmond

Track 158

Swing

mf

pp

Performance Pieces

You've Made It!

Now you've learned all the main concepts of music reading, it's time to put everything into practice. This final section of the book presents pieces and songs that you can perform to your friends and family, or simply play for your own pleasure.

The Pedals

As you start to play proper pieces and full songs you will need to get acquainted with the pedals.

The Sustaining Pedal

When you put your foot on the sustaining pedal the rack of dampers is moved away from the strings, enabling them to vibrate freely. There is nothing to stop the sound, even when you take your finger off the key. Try it now: Put the pedal down and play several notes. The instrument sustains the sound until it decays gradually over time. This is a useful effect, enabling you to maintain the sound of a bass note underneath changing melody notes, or help with legato passages. Above all it enriches the tone of the instrument, adding "color" to the sound.

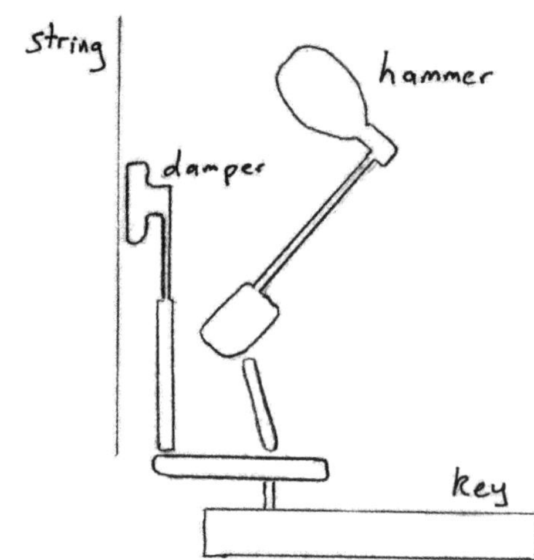

The Soft Pedal

The soft pedal, or **una corda** ("one string" in Italian), also alters the tone. On a grand piano, it shifts the entire action of the keyboard to the right so that the hammers only strike one of the strings in each note, as opposed to all three. This will produce a softer sound. On upright pianos, the effect is produced in a different way: The rack of hammers is moved closer to the strings, so that they can't hit the strings with as much force. Experiment with this pedal by playing some of the pieces you have learnt so far with the pedal down in select passages. Notice the softer tone.

"Moonlit Pagoda" by Denes Agay is a good piece for using the pedals. The pedal markings underneath the bass clef staff indicate when you should lift the (sustaining) pedal, which is generally at the end of a phrase. It might be an idea to use the soft pedal, too, in order to achieve a gentle tone.

Practice without pedals first to get used to the notes. The piece is easier than it looks! It is in the difficult key of G♭ major, but it is played entirely on black keys. It is slow. Once you have mastered the notes, try using the pedal and enjoy the colors achieved by merging tones together. From measure 17 to the end, you should play all notes with upward stems with your right hand and all notes with downward stems with the left hand.

The Basics
Time Signature: 3/4 (three quarter notes per measure)
Starts on: First beat. Count, "1, 2, 3, 4, 5," and then play.
Key: G♭ major (B♭, E♭, A♭, D♭, G♭, and C♭ in the key signature)
Right Hand: G♭ above middle C
Left Hand: G♭ and D♭ around middle C

MOONLIT PAGODA

By Denes Agay

I Giorni, by modern Italian composer Ludovico Einaudi, makes use of both the sustaining pedal and the soft pedal.

Drills

Play through the main left-hand motif. You need to stretch your fingers right out in the third measure. Here, you should put down the sustaining pedal and let it hold the sound for another full measure. If you do this correctly, you should be able to hear all three notes clearly, as though they form a chord.

 *Track 160*

Next, play through this left-hand motif. The shape of each measure is exactly the same; you just need to move your hand to the right place at the start of each measure. Use the same fingering for each one, and try to play this as smoothly as you can.

Track 161

Now try this passage with your right hand. Place a slight emphasis on the marked top notes. When you put this together with the left hand it might feel as if you're playing cross-rhythms, as you have two phrases of three eighth notes in each measure over the top of three quarter notes in the left hand.

Track 162

Finally let's look at the last chord in the piece. The squiggly line means you should play a rolled chord; start at the bottom and play each note in sequence up to the top, holding each one down as you go.

Track 163

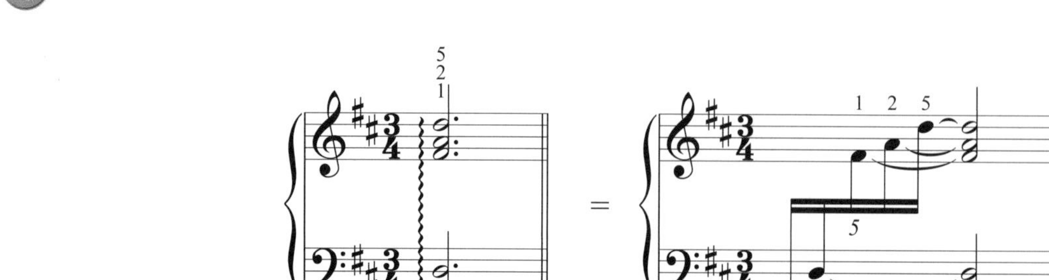

The Basics
Time Signature: 3/4 (three quarter notes per measure)
Starts on: First beat. Count, "1, 2, 3," and then play.
Key: B minor (F♯ and C♯ in the key signature)
Right Hand: D over an octave above middle C
Left Hand: B below middle C

I GIORNI

By Ludovico Einaudi

Track 164

Ped.
Ped.
Ped.
With pedal

3
5 1 2
mp
5 5
4
5
5
2
1
3
5 1 3
cresc.
2
2
2 3
mf
1 2
cresc.
5 2 1
f
5
2
1

Gizeh is by modern German composer Oskar Schuster. It is in a minor key but without a key signature. The 3/4 time evokes the idea of a waltz, and the left hand echoes some notes from the right-hand melody line. The hands are spaced quite far apart because the right hand plays the entire piece an octave higher than the printed notes. This is indicated by the **8va** sign above the treble staff, and it makes reading the notes easier.

Track 165

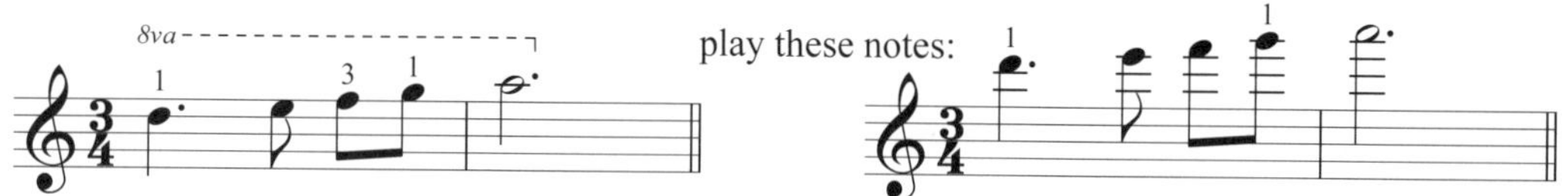

You will need to spend some time practicing the left hand on its own. Notice how it starts in the bass clef but is up in the treble clef for the whole of the last three lines.

The geography of the piece also needs some attention: There are three repeats, and the second one has first- and second-time measures. After measure 25, there is a **D.C. al Coda**. This means you should go back to the beginning, and at the end of measure 17 (second time), you go to the coda.

The Basics
Time Signature: 3/4 (three quarter notes per measure)
Starts on: First beat. Count, "1, 2, 3," and then play.
Key: D minor (no key signature)
Right Hand: D over two octaves above middle C
Left Hand: D above middle C

GIZEH

By Oskar Schuster

Track 166

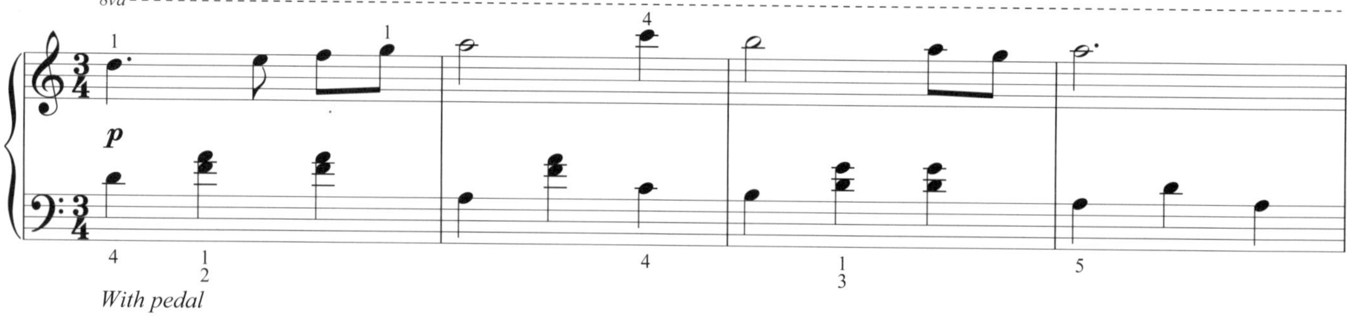

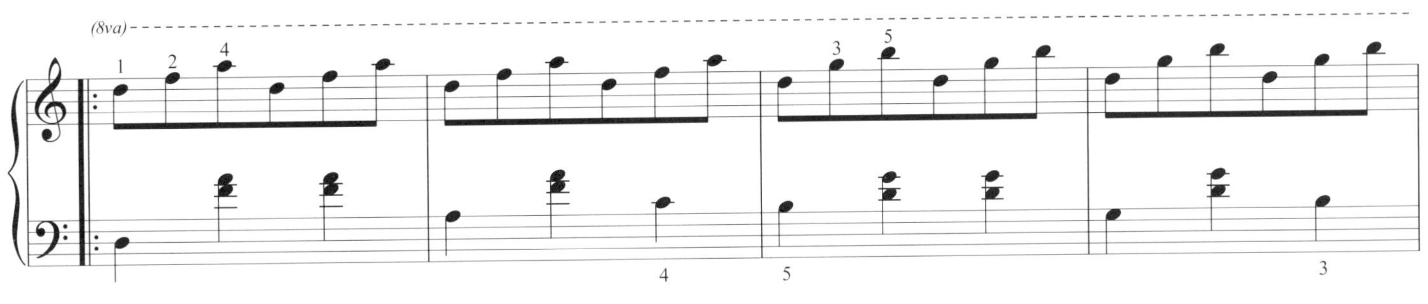
(8va)

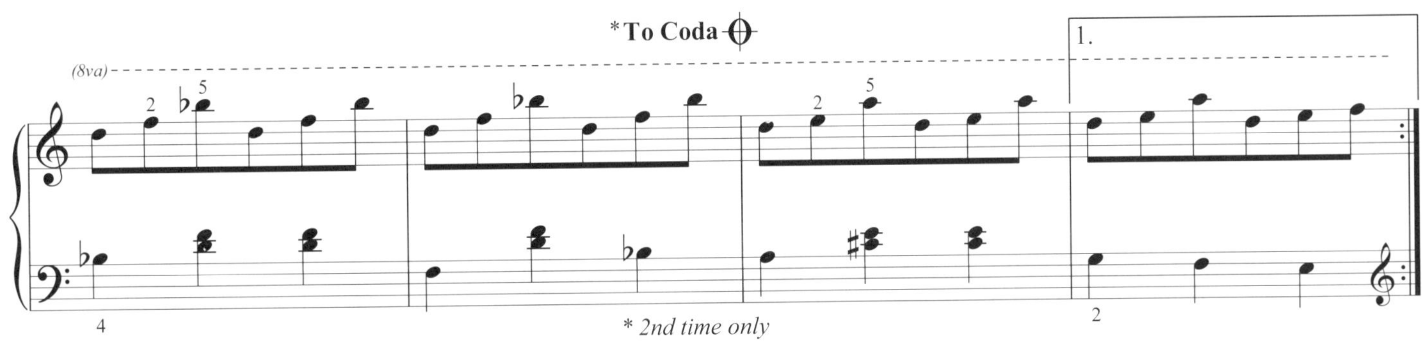
*To Coda
(8va)
1.
* 2nd time only

2.
(8va)

(8va)
1.
2.
(8va)

D.C. al Coda
(8va)
CODA
(8va)
rit.

"Comptine D'un Autre Ete" by Yann Tiersen comes from the film *Amélie*. It is in a minor key and has a repetitive left-hand theme running throughout the piece.

Drills

Try playing through the left-hand motif. You need to stretch out to a full octave. It will help if you move your elbow from side to side as you play; move to the right on the B and then back to the left on the next B a beat later. This way, the arm movement can help the fingers. Try to keep this smooth.

Track 167

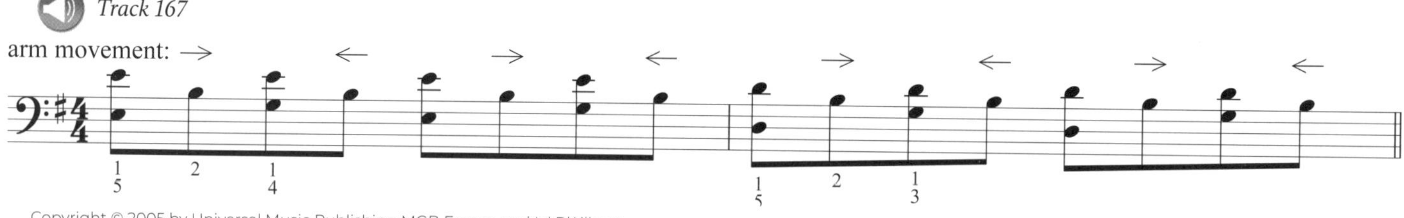

At measure 17, you have a tricky passage of 16th notes in the right hand played over the top of the same left-hand motif. It's tricky because the three-note cuts across the eighth-note sequence in the left hand. As you play the right hand, try to give a little extra emphasis on the marked notes, which fall in line with the beats.

Track 168

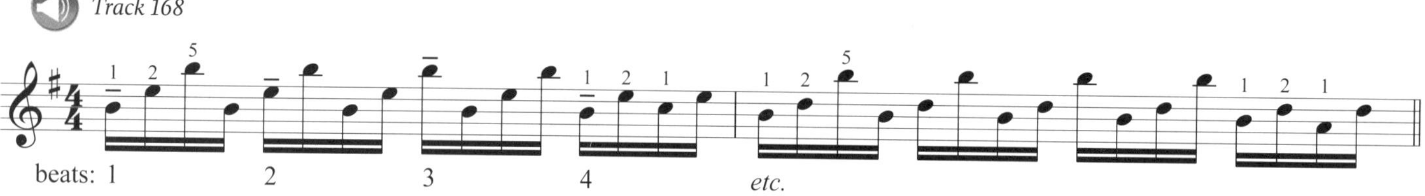

> **The Basics**
> **Time Signature:** 4/4 (four quarter notes per measure)
> **Starts on:** First beat. Count, "1, 2, 3, 4," and then play.
> **Key:** E minor (F# in the key signature)
> **Right Hand:** G above middle C
> **Left Hand:** An octave—E and E around middle C

COMPTINE D'UN AUTRE ÉTÉ: L'APRÈS-MIDI

(from *Amélie*)

By Yann Tiersen

Track 169

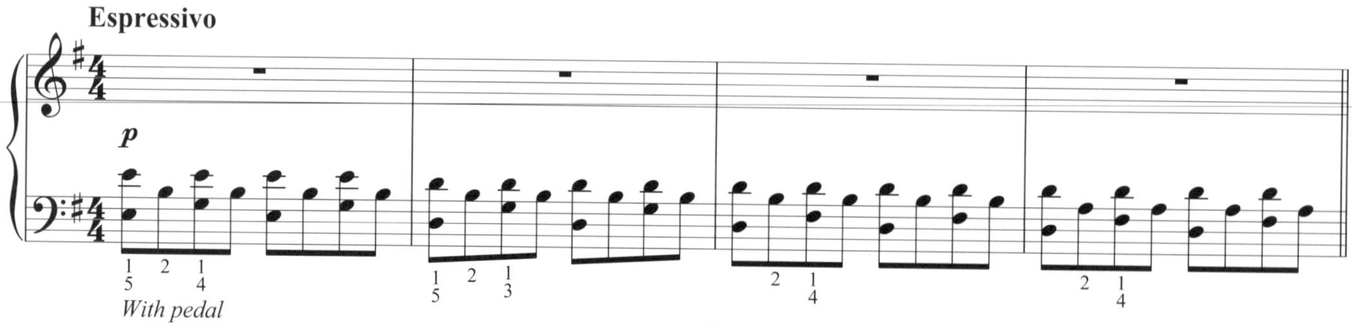

mp
p
mf
1.
2.
rit.
p a tempo

8va
mf
(8va)
1.
(8va)
2.
rit.
pp

The Second Voice

Leading on from playing chords is the concept of the second voice, which is essentially two lines happening simultaneously in one hand.

Look at the following exercises for the right hand. In the first one, there are quarter notes in the upper voice, but you need to hold down a whole note with your thumb at the same time. This is the **lower** or **second voice**. It's very easy to forget the lower voice and accidentally take your thumb off the C. You must endeavor to continue holding it down so that you can hear it right at the end of the measure.

Track 170

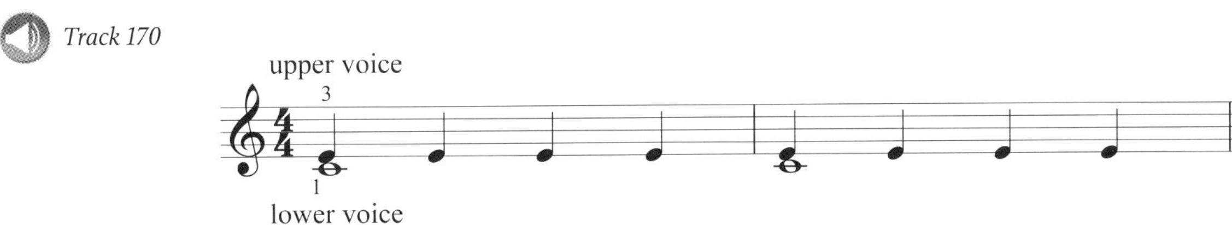

Now let's make it more complicated: The lower voice has more to do in the second measure while the upper voice simply holds down the E.

Track 171

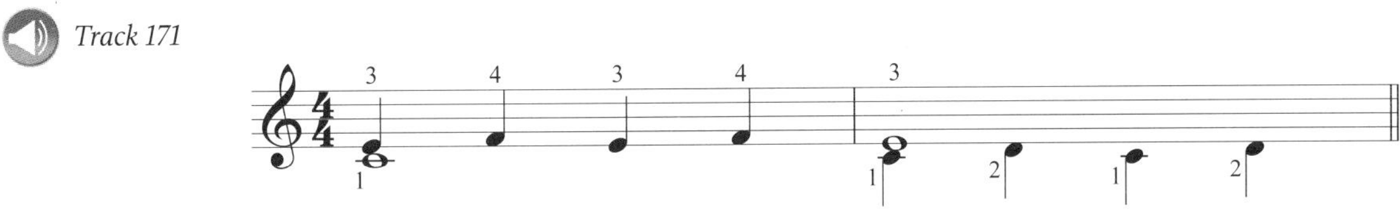

Left-Hand Drills

"Old French Song" by Tchaikovsky makes use of a second voice in the left hand. Play through the upper voice on its own first, accounting for the key signature—you use both flats in the first three measures.

Track 172

By Pyotr Il'yich Tchaikovsky

Now add in the lower voice. You need to hold down the G with the fifth finger. The final note here belongs to both voices, indicated by two opposing stems on a single note head.

Track 173

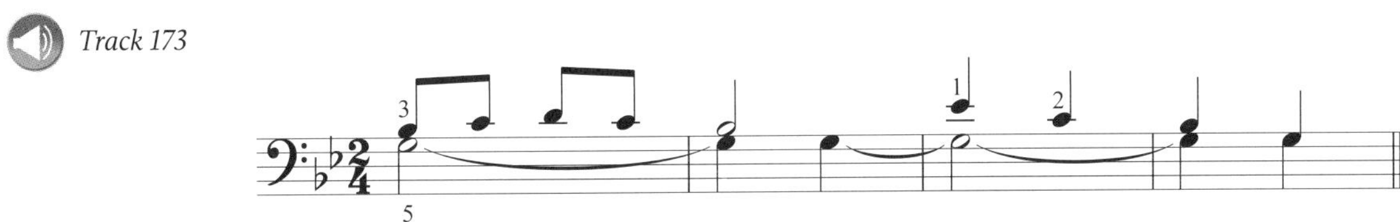

It's worth practicing this tricky passage too. Here, you should play the eighth notes in a detached style, but don't take the staccato dots too literally—keep it gentle. Decide which fingering you like best in the first measure and stick to it.

Track 174

Right-Hand Drill

Here the right hand has two voices. You need to hold down the upper-voice A over the changing lower voice. To understand the tricky dotted rhythm in the upper voice, you should subdivide the second beat into four equal parts. The dotted eighth note occupies the first three and the 16th note is the fourth.

Track 175

The Basics

Time Signature: 2/4 (two quarter notes per measure)
Starts on: Second half of second beat. Count, "1 and 2," and then play.
Key: G minor (B♭ and E♭ in the key signature)
Right Hand: D above middle C
Left Hand: G and B♭ below middle C

OLD FRENCH SONG, OP. 39, NO. 16

(from *Album for the Young, Op. 39*)

By Pyotr Il'yich Tchaikovsky

Track 176

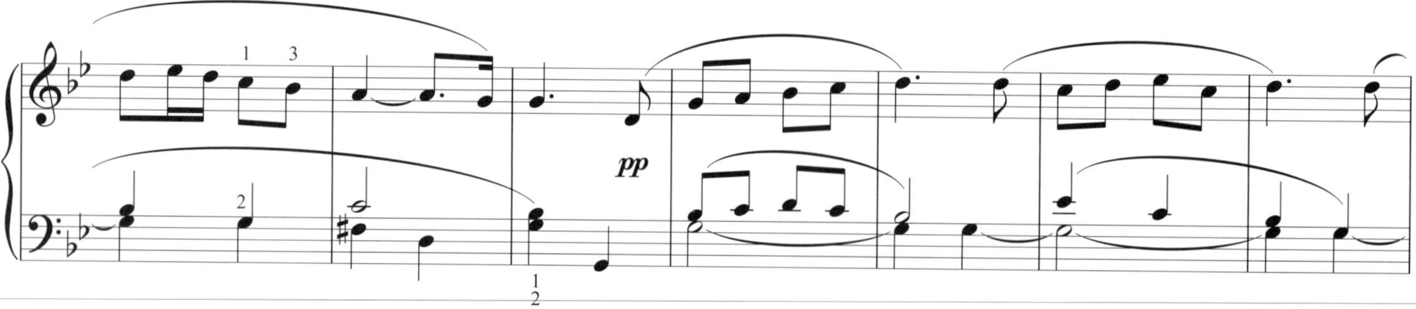

Finishing on a positive note, the last song in the book is "Happy" by Pharrell Williams.

Syncopation

There are occasional examples of this in other songs we've covered, but this song has **syncopation** in abundance. A syncopated rhythm has a lot of off-beats: notes that fall directly on the half beat. They are often accented to give the rhythm an off-center groove.

The example below has all notes off the beat. Try playing the upper notes (on any one note of the piano) while tapping the lower beats with your left hand. Then, drop out the left hand and just *feel* the pulse underneath.

Track 177

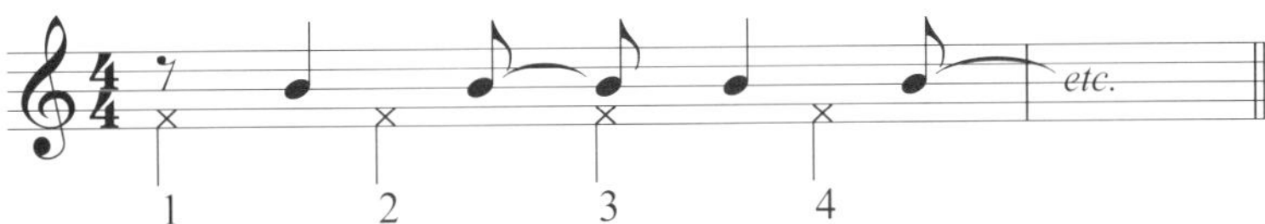

Now here's the chorus from the song. Play the lower voice notes first to get the hang of the syncopated rhythm. This is of course the main vocal line of the chorus. Then, add in the upper voice. This is the "backing vocal" and should be a lot softer than the lower voice. This is difficult to achieve!

Track 178

The Basics
Time Signature: 4/4 (four quarter notes per measure)
Starts on: First beat. Count, "1, 2, 3, 4," and then play.
Key: E minor (F# in the key signature)
Right Hand: D and G# above middle C
Left Hand: E and B below middle C

HAPPY

(from *Despicable Me 2*)

Words and Music by Pharrell Williams

Track 179

mf

Appendix 1
Diagram of a Piano

UPRIGHT PIANO

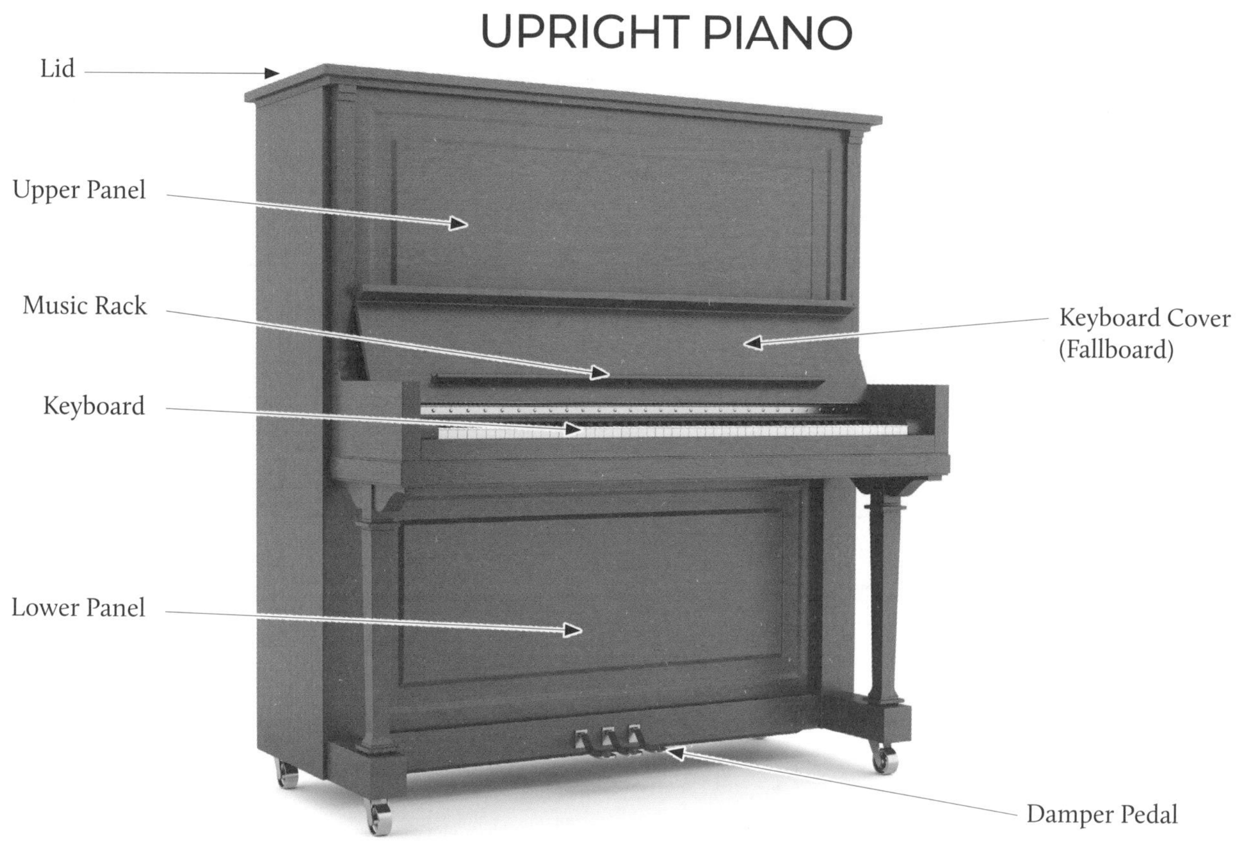

GRAND PIANO

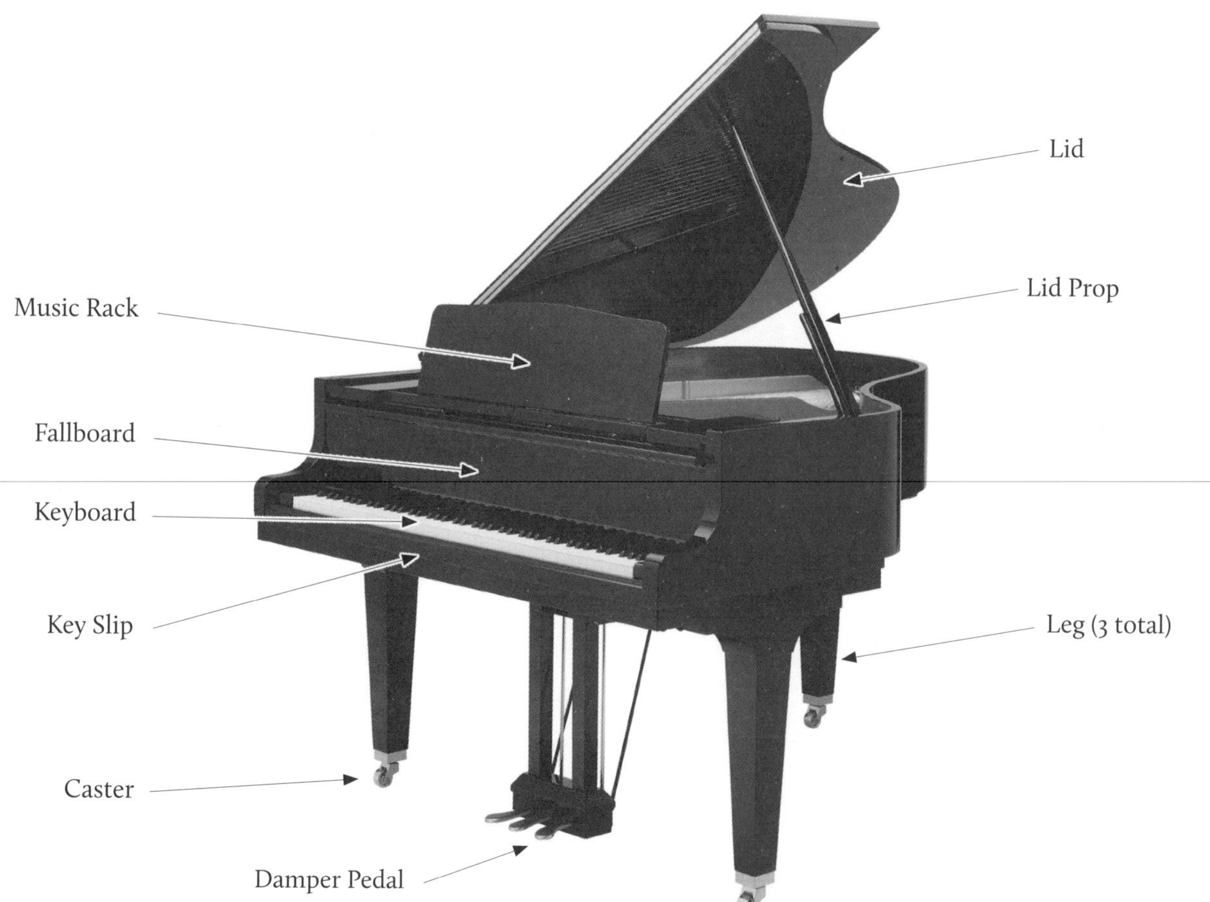

Appendix 2

Chord Table

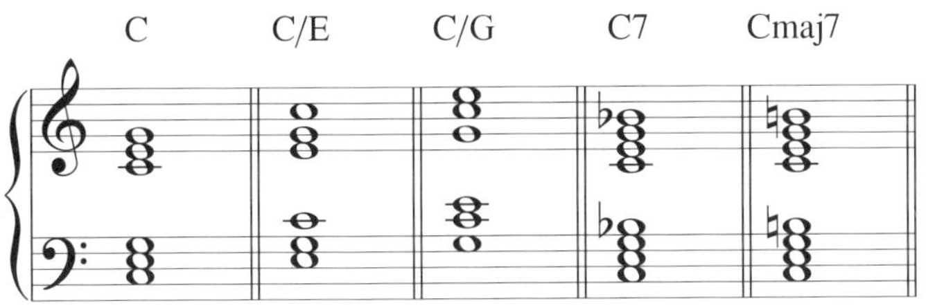

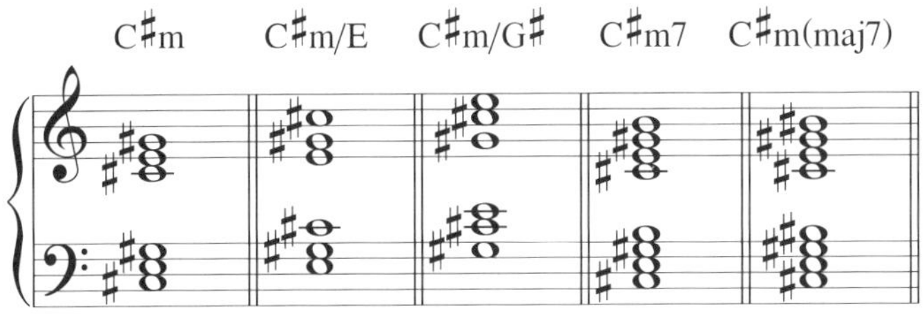

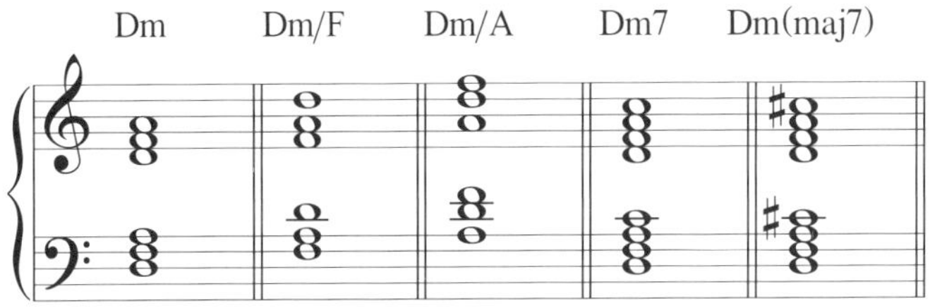

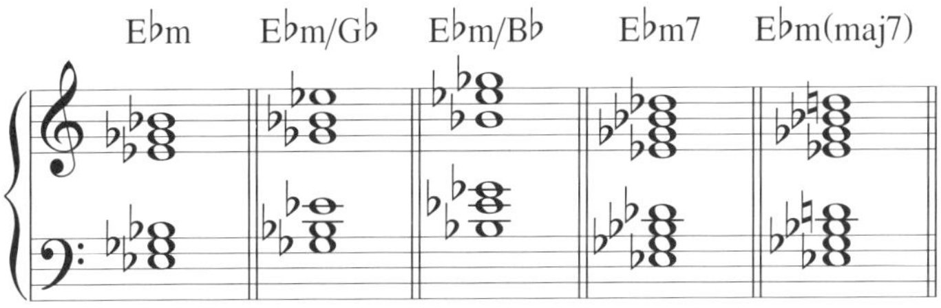

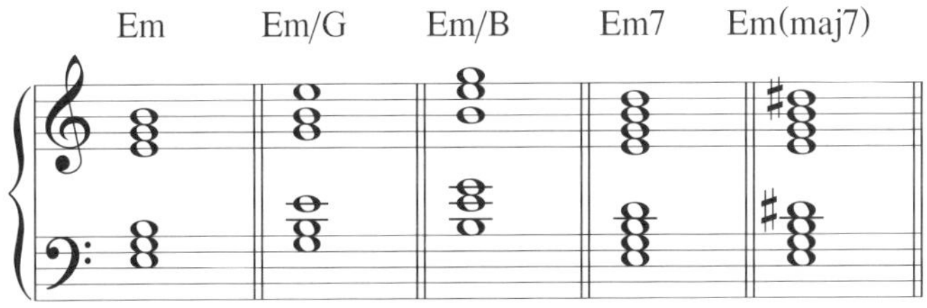

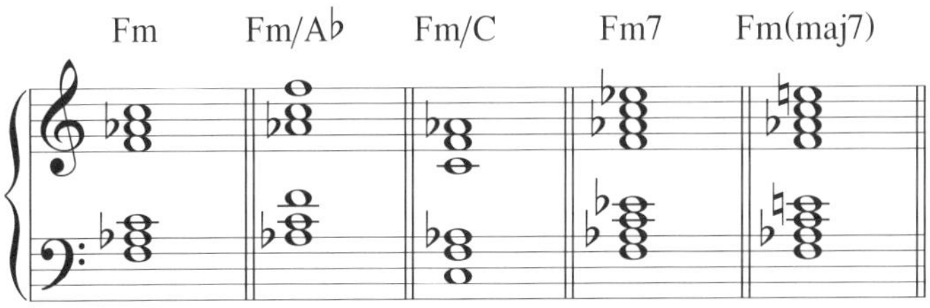

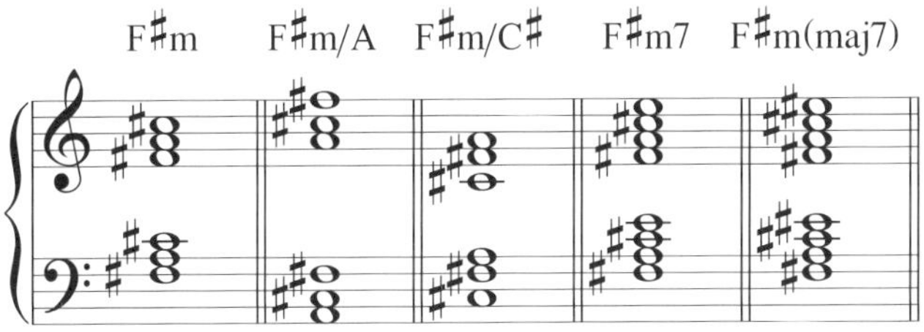

C C/E C/G C7 Cmaj7

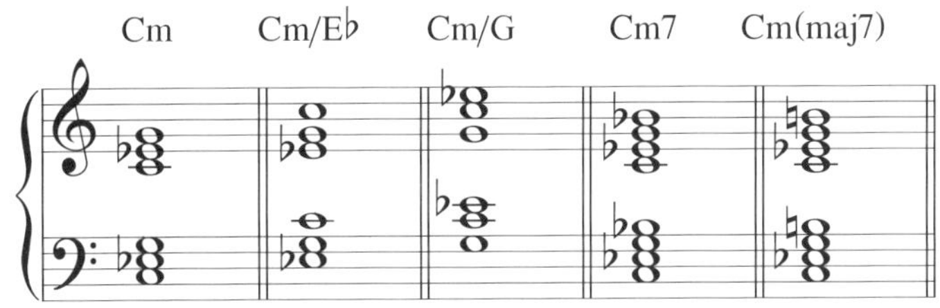

D♭ D♭/F D♭/A♭ D♭7 D♭maj7

D D/F♯ D/A D7 Dmaj7

E♭ E♭/G E♭/B♭ E♭7 E♭maj7

E E/G♯ E/B E7 Emaj7

F F/A F/C F7 Fmaj7

F♯ F♯/A♯ F♯/C♯ F♯7 F♯maj7

Cm Cm/E♭ Cm/G Cm7 Cm(maj7)

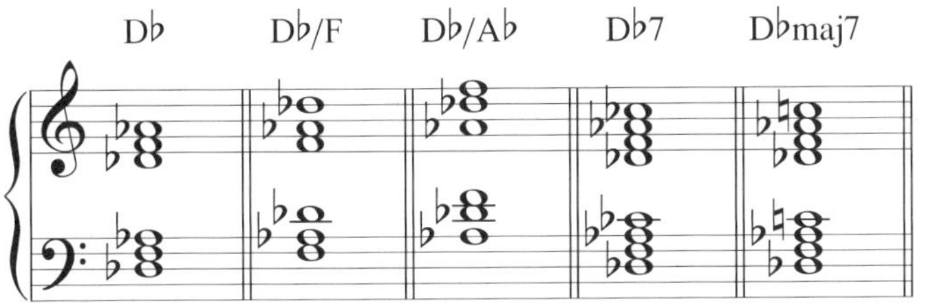

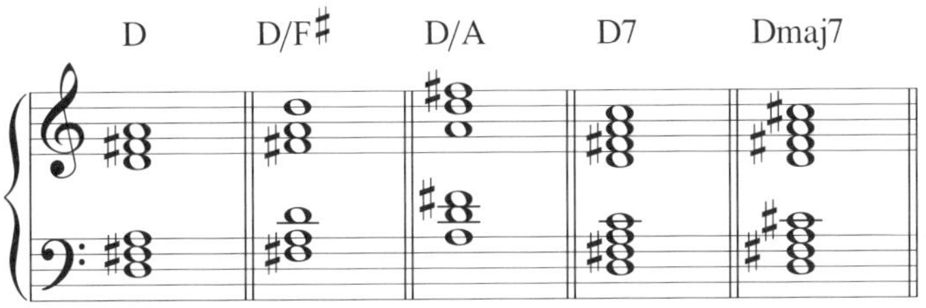

C♯m C♯m/E C♯m/G♯ C♯m7 C♯m(maj7)

Dm Dm/F Dm/A Dm7 Dm(maj7)

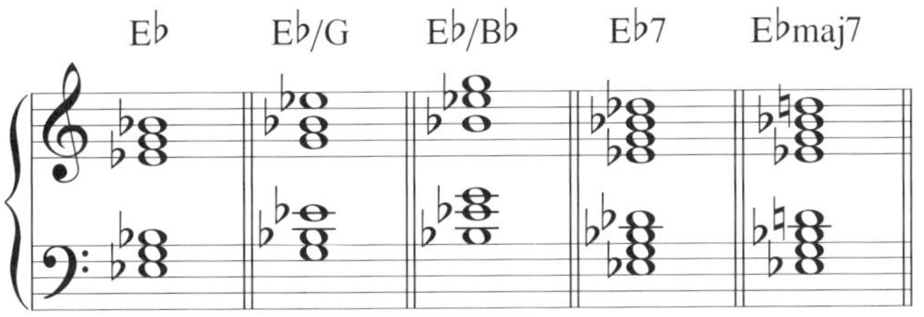

E♭m E♭m/G♭ E♭m/B♭ E♭m7 E♭m(maj7)

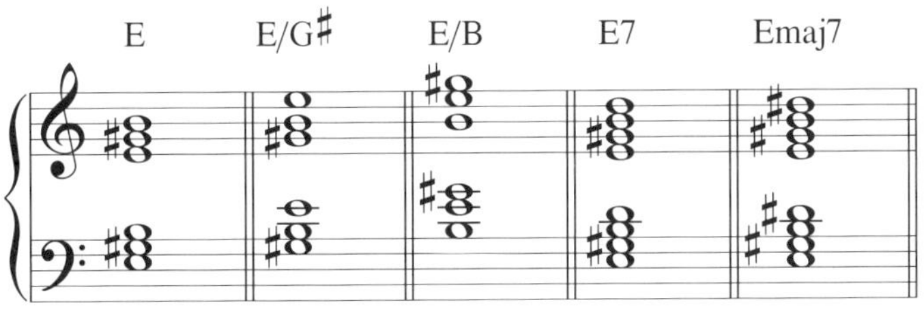

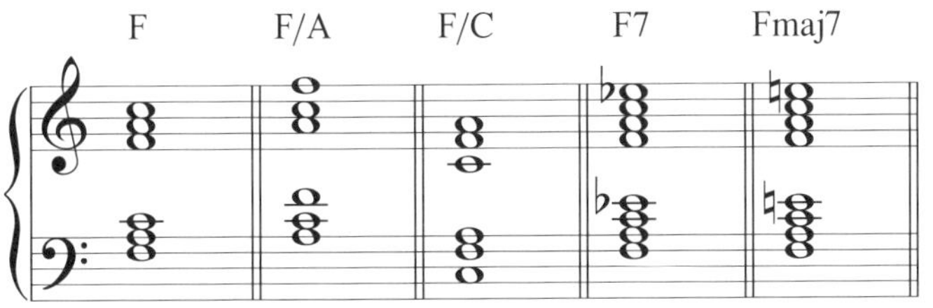

Em Em/G Em/B Em7 Em(maj7)

Fm Fm/A♭ Fm/C Fm7 Fm(maj7)

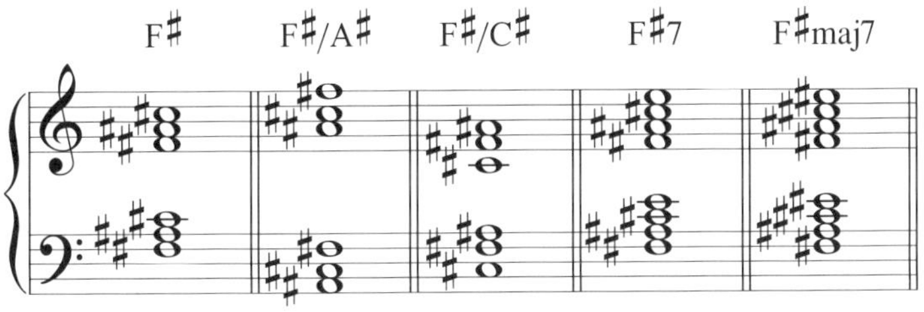

F♯m F♯m/A F♯m/C♯ F♯m7 F♯m(maj7)

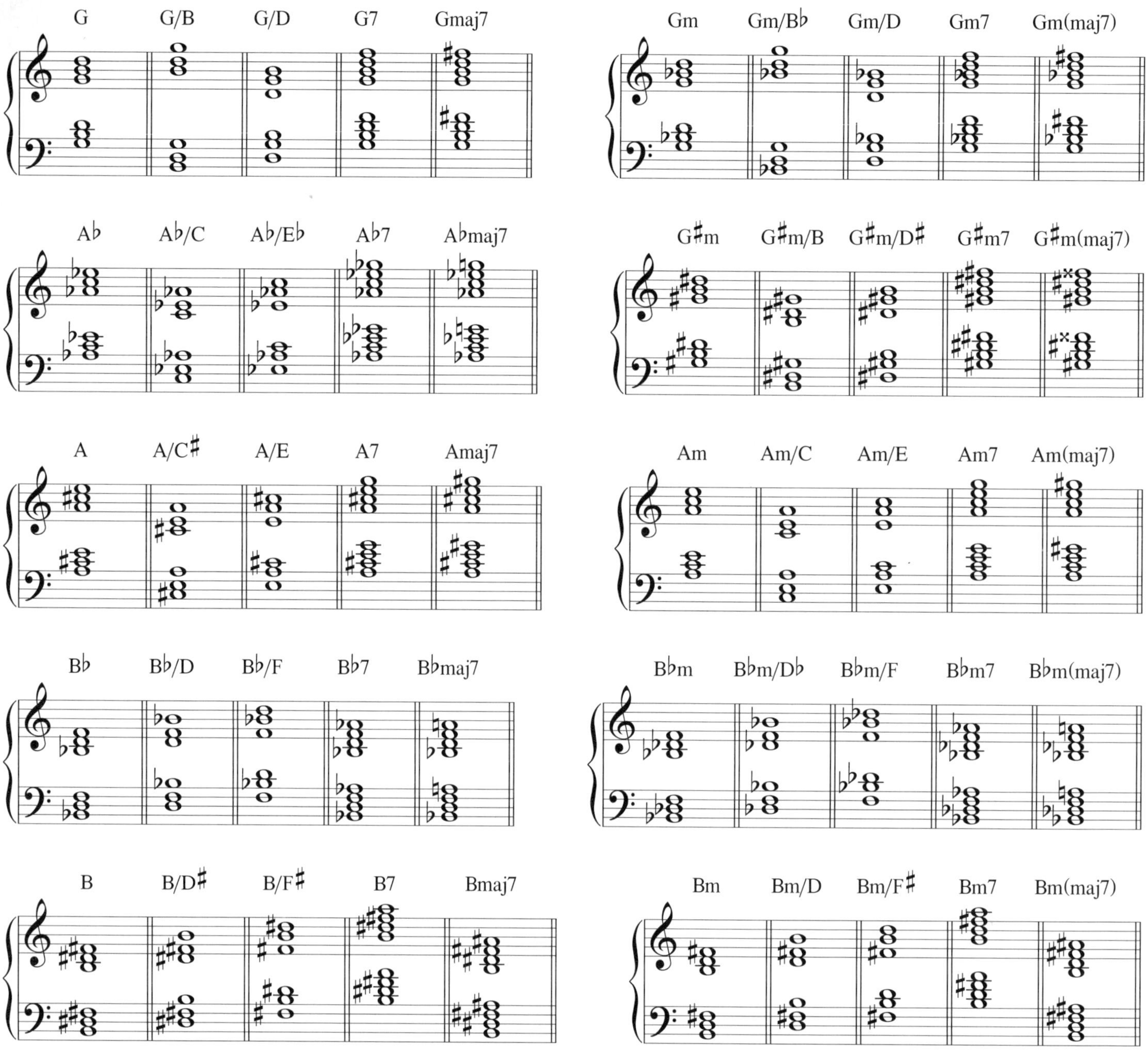
G
G/B
G/D
G7
Gmaj7
Gm
Gm/B♭
Gm/D
Gm7
Gm(maj7)
A♭
A♭/C
A♭/E♭
A♭7
A♭maj7
G♯m
G♯m/B
G♯m/D♯
G♯m7
G♯m(maj7)
A
A/C♯
A/E
A7
Amaj7
Am
Am/C
Am/E
Am7
Am(maj7)
B♭
B♭/D
B♭/F
B♭7
B♭maj7
B♭m
B♭m/D♭
B♭m/F
B♭m7
B♭m(maj7)
B
B/D♯
B/F♯
B7
Bmaj7
Bm
Bm/D
Bm/F♯
Bm7
Bm(maj7)

Key Signatures

C major
A minor
G major
E minor
D major
B minor
A major
F♯ minor
E major
C♯ minor
B major
G♯ minor
C♯ major
A♯ minor
F major
D minor
B♭ major
G minor
E♭ major
C minor
A♭ major
F minor
D♭ major
B♭ minor
C♭ major
A♭ minor

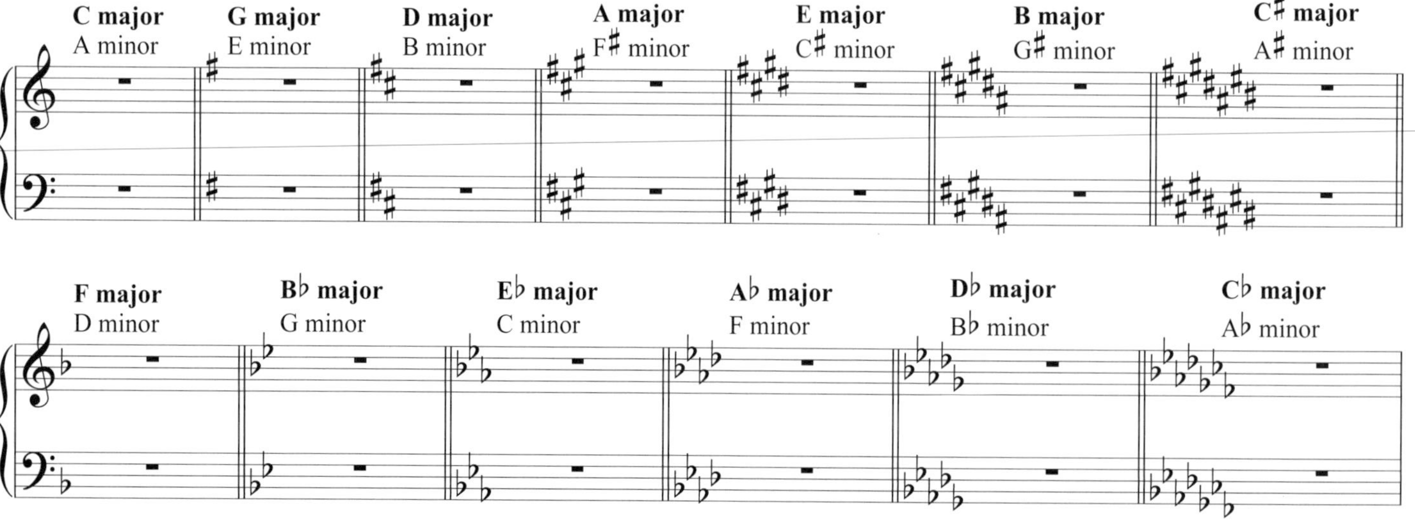